NOV   9 1981

School Vandalism

School Vandalism

Strategies for Prevention

Michael D. Casserly
The Council of the
Great City Schools

Scott A. Bass
Centre Research, Inc.

John R. Garrett
Vladeck, Hinds and Garrett Inc.

LexingtonBooks
D.C. Heath and Company
Lexington, Massachusetts
Toronto

Library of Congress Cataloging in Publication Data

Casserly, Michael D.
    School vandalism.

    Bibliography: p.
    1. School vandalism. I. Bass, Scott A., joint author. II Garrett,
John R., joint author. III. Title.
LB 3249.C37   371.5'8   80-8118
ISBN 0-669-03956-x

Copyright © 1980 by D.C. Heath and Company

Published simultaneously in Canada

Printed in the United States of America

International Standard Book Number: 0-669-03956-x

Library of Congress Catalog Card Number: 80-8118

Contents

Preface   vii

Acknowledgments   xi

Chapter 1   **Overview: Theory and Definitions**   1

Understanding School Vandalism   2
Defining Vandalism   4
Approaches—Not Answers   8

Chapter 2   **A Review of the Research**   11

Extent of School Vandalism   11
Trends in School Vandalism   13
Targets of School Vandalism   14
Nature of School Vandalism   15
The Vandals   15
When Does the Destruction Occur?   17
Where Does the Destruction Occur?   17
The Schools   18
What Do We Need to Know?   20
Summary   21

Chapter 3   **School Vandalism: An Analysis of Major Options**   23

Building-Security Programs   24
Target-Hardening Programs   36
Architectural-Design Programs   38
Offender-Accountability Programs   39
Behavioral-Change Programs   41
Human-Relations Programs   43
Community-Relations Programs   45
Institutional-Change Programs   46
Curriculum-Innovation Programs   47
Summary   49

Chapter 4   **Case Studies of Prevention Programs**   51

Fresno County, California   52
Flint, Michigan   54
Madison, Wisconsin   56

	Dallas, Texas	58
	Alexandria, Virginia	61
	Escambia County, Florida	63
	Summary	65

Chapter 5	Designing a School-Vandalism-Prevention Program	67
	Problem Assessment	67
	Resource Identification	76
	Program Planning	78
	Program Evaluation	85
	Summary	87

| Chapter 6 | Summary and Conclusions | 89 |

| Appendix A | Resource Guide | 95 |

| Appendix B | Sample Security/Vandalism Report Forms: General | 109 |

| Appendix C | Security/Vandalism Report Forms for Specific Areas | 127 |

| | Bibliography | 137 |

| | Index | 160 |

| | The Council of the Great City Schools | 164 |

| | About the Authors | 166 |

Preface

In 1976 we approached the Council of the Great City Schools about writing a handbook for school administrators on controlling vandalism. At the time the seriousness of the problem had far outstripped the literature and the confidence of school people to deal effectively with the destruction. A number of local studies had been done on the extent of the ruination, and the Senate subcommittee study had just been released on the horrors of everyday life in the nation's public schools. The press was publishing on an almost daily basis information on the enormous cost in dollars, lives, and learning that vandalism entailed. Associations and academics alike began to ask what had gone wrong. Were schools really so horrid that they could be compared with prisons? Were the teen years to be written off as a passing demographic blip unfortunately characterized by senseless violence? And what of the mayhem depicted on television and in the movies and its effect on the young? Was society simply reaping the spoiled fruit grown from bad seeds? It was not long before every thread in the schools' institutional fabric was being questioned. Actually, the questioning came long before and had its most immediate roots in the unrest of the 1960s. But the raucous behavior of that decade cannot satisfactorily explain why schools were being burned. There were places that were never touched. And the traditional sociological and psychological theories appeared impotent to add an illuminating idea.

And what has happened since then? The papers and the national newsweeklies no longer run nonstop articles on sixth-graders pillaging the local junior high. The problem in many communities has not abated, however. What has changed dramatically is the attention of the American people. Violence and vandalism in schools are not the exotic status-laden fields they once were, despite the continuation of the destruction. They no longer capture our imaginations nor horrify our sensibilities. Schools are still gutted dramatically and nibbled at slowly. Since the mid-1970s a number of important works have been published including the *Safe School Study* and books by Rubel, and Vestermark and Blauvelt, and others. The work of these and other writers should be acknowledged here for continuing to focus our fickle attention on a serious problem. And the schools themselves deserve special praise for their innovation and quiet resolve in dealing with a situation that in many ways is not of their own creation. Many would be genuinely surprised at the sensitivity and commitment poured into the development of local programs. Although the cameras were not rolling, these people continued to experiment and study to come up with effective strategies.

For years, educators have been attempting a host of approaches to curbing vandalism, some more successful than others. Nowhere at the time we started this work, however, was there a single source that could add some coherence to an increasing number of theories, studies, approaches, and resources. It was this gap in the literature, the needs of the schools, and the Council's own leadership that compelled the Council to embark on a project to bring together what was known about vandalism and to contribute to the burgeoning field. The final report of that project formed the basis for this book. It was the commitment of the Council of the Great City Schools to quality education that ultimately gave birth to an idea too long gravid.

What we have attempted to do in this work is twofold. First, we have tried to compile the major theories and research bearing on school vandalism and the most significant strategies for dealing with it. We are indebted to those who have supplied articles and leads through the years to make this compilation possible. The major themes and patterns in the literature are highlighted throughout the text. Second, we have attempted to put vandalism prevention into a strictly educational context. It was our conviction—as it was the conviction of many—that good schooling was made of more than the absence of chaos. Still needed were security programs that complemented the long-range goals of our educational system: a literate and productive citizenry. To do this we include a chapter that outlines a process for schools to consider in treating their vandalism problem. Although the book contains a number of practical strategies as the title suggests, it is not a catalog. Nor does it offer any definitive programs or prescriptions. What it does provide is a context for current thinking about the incidence of vandalism and its prevention.

The first chapter of this book presents an overview of school vandalism. The federal involvement in the field is summarized, and the various theories from which current vandalism theory emerged are described. Finally, the chapter presents a review of current definitions of vandalism and the assumptions inherent throughout the book.

Chapter 2 presents an overview of the research on school vandalism. The chapter reviews the major national studies that have examined the trends in school vandalism and explored characteristics of vandals, of the schools that suffer most, and of the destructive act itself.

Chapter 3 categorizes and describes the major kinds of vandalism-prevention programs in schools today. These include those oriented toward building security, target hardening, architectural change, offender accountability, behavioral change, human relations, community relations, institutional change, and curriculum innovation. Within each category, we discuss how widely the approach is used, describe some of its salient features, and suggest what to consider when selecting a program.

Chapter 4 examines the school vandalism programs in Fresno County, California; Flint, Michigan; Dallas, Texas; Madison, Wisconsin; Alexandria, Virginia; and Escambia County, Florida. Each of these districts illustrates various preventive efforts at work.

Chapter 5 outlines a strategy for use at the local district level to assess the seriousness and extent of the problem, to appraise various program options, to estimate how much the program might cost, to plan for the resources needed, to implement the program and to evaluate its success.

Chapter 6 summarizes the work that has been covered and draws a number of conclusions in the areas of program planning, data analysis, project management, and others.

In addition appendixes are provided that include an annotated "shopping list" of some of the resources we encountered in working on this book that may be of value in planning a local project. Also included are a number of sample instruments for reporting vandalism at both the building and central-office level. An extensive bibliography on school vandalism follows this appendix.

Acknowledgments

We are grateful to a number of friends and colleagues who helped in various ways to make this book a reality. First and foremost, we would like to thank Milton Bins, senior associate at the Council of the Great City Schools. Without his vision and leadership, the project culminating in this book would never have gotten off the ground. Throughout the course of the work, he was forced to draw on an endless reserve of patience with his often-cantankerous authors. It was Milton who helped us see the problem as more than broken windows but as a crisis contributing to the public's waning confidence in the schools. And we would like to thank Samuel Husk, executive director of the Council, for his leadership in this effort and his perseverence in the face of what must have seemed an endless task. We would also like to extend our appreciation to those who reviewed the work in its various stages: Peter Blauvelt, William Gaymon, Donald Johnson, Curt Lamb, Michael Marvin, Donald McElroy, Jane Mercer, Cecil Middleton, John Minor, Charles O'Toole, Suzanne Piscitello, Stanley Rideout, and Mania Seferi. In addition, chapter 4 would not be what it is without the diligence and contributions of Bruce Astrein. And finally we are indebted to our editor Margaret Zusky for steering us through the publishing labyrinth.

1

Overview: Theory and Definitions

Nearly thirty years ago, an important study of the maladjusted child concluded that stealing and rowdyism were the most serious acts of student indiscretion schools were ever likely to face (Morgan 1952). And as recently as 1957 Sheldon and Eleanor Glueck included on their list of student misbehaviors such violations as persistent inattention, carelessness, underhandedness, and smoking. Clearly, things have changed. For many school systems across the country, violence and vandalism are issues of major concern.

Student disruptions are not unique to the last twenty-five years, of course. In other times, and in other places, school-aged children and young adults have attacked their peers, teachers, and physical surroundings. In the period after 1790, the house owned by the president of Brown College was stoned nightly, food riots and dueling were common at Harvard, and the first murder of a professor by a disgruntled North Carolina student occurred (Kett 1977). Not until the late 1800s, however, following the first large waves of immigration did serious social concern turn to the conduct of teenagers. By 1870 the first settlement houses were being founded to provide shelter for homeless children and to free the city streets from the prowling bands of youngsters bent on developing what was seen as their natural criminal instincts (Asbury 1928). But the distasteful acts of these young people were considered rare, isolated in individuals who were seen by peers and professionals alike as aberrant and disturbed.

Today, however, disruptions of one sort or another are experienced in schools—once considered exempt from threatening and destructive behavior—as part of the expected day-to-day educational routine. Educators have always been quick to point out that schools mirrored the society around them, for better or for worse, but few anticipated that America's violence would be reflected within the classrooms. Like churches, schools had traditionally been viewed as a haven from the disorders of everyday life.

Because of the attention paid to school violence in the last ten to fifteen years—in the form of innumerable articles, studies, and hearings—it has become difficult to separate true increases in disruptive behavior from changes in our sensitivity and awareness of it. The studies embraced a panorama of approaches and methodologies and arrived at diverse recommendations and conclusions. This diversity has been healthy and productive, but it has been accompanied, as well, by a scale of quality and methodological precision that runs from excellent to abominable. At the national level, inconsistencies in sampling and reporting school violence have caused considerable uncertainty about the true nature and extent of the problem.

1

To address that uncertainty, the federal government has been very active over the years. Its involvement in the delinquency problem, in general, dates to the early 1950s when the U.S. Senate Committee on the Judiciary established a Subcommittee on Juvenile Delinquency. That Subcommittee's early attention was focused on the disruption in schools following the forced desegregation of southern districts. In 1961 the first major piece of federal legislation was seen— the Juvenile Delinquency and Youth Offenses Control Act—designed to prevent youth crime through a series of training and demonstration programs. By 1967 not only had the government initiated and conducted a wide-ranging study under the direction of the President's Commission on Law Enforcement and the Administration of Justice but the courts were beginning to rule on a host of due-process cases for juveniles.

Rising crime levels, especially in urban areas, brought the passage in 1968 of both the Juvenile Delinquency Prevention and Control Act and The Omnibus Crime Control and Safe Streets Act, but it was not until the latter's reauthorization in 1973 that congressional attention began to focus on the connection between crime and schools. In the following year, two landmark bills were passed: the 1974 Amendments to the Elementary and Secondary Education Act and the Juvenile Justice and Delinquency Prevention Act. The former provided the authorization for the important *Safe School Study* (1977) and the latter instituted a host of efforts to coordinate delinquency programs throughout the federal government. As the *Safe School Study* was getting under way, the Senate Subcommittee on Juvenile Delinquency completed its lengthy and controversial hearings and studies on the extent and nature of school crime. Not until the Safe School Study was finished, however, did some of the uncertainty over the extent of the problem dissipate. Its best evidence appears to indicate that school-crime got steadily worse through the 1960s and early 1970s but has leveled off— maybe even decreased— since then. Unfortunately, no one really knows what aspects of the problem have changed, or why.

Understanding School Vandalism

Vandalism is not distinct, by and large, from theories of juvenile delinquency. Many view property destruction among youth as simply one manifestation of the larger delinquency problem. The fact that vandalism costs so much and is so visible, however, gives the field a certain uniqueness within the literature.

There are, in general, two basic approaches to understanding vandalism: the first emphasizes individual characteristics of the vandal, and the second focuses on broader societal problems. The first finds its roots in the early epidemiological studies of youth and crime that began in the 1920s; including studies by Beccavia on the pleasure and pain thresholds in criminals; Lombroso's examinations of criminal physiology; and analyses by Kertschmer, Glueck, and Sheldon on body types. All assumed that the source of deviant behavior could be found in the physical makeup of the individual. The individualist tradition also influenced the many psychiatric and psychoanalytic studies of delinquency. In his classic *Wayward Youth* (1931) for instance, August Aichorn concludes that delinquency could be traced to the interplay of "dissocial" psychic forces. More recently, Juillerat (1966) has suggested that much of the crime in schools could be laid at the feet of emotionally disturbed young people. McPartland and McDill (1977) have argued against this approach in claiming that the small numbers of disturbed youngsters could not possibly account for all the destruction.

The modern correllary to the individual approach is found in current studies on the genetic composition of delinquents and on physiologically based learning disabilities. This latter approach has received considerable play in the literature, but the evidence supporting the notion that juvenile delinquency, violence, and vandalism are linked to learning disabilities is scanty (Murray 1976). Still, anecdotal evidence lends some credence to the possibility that some vandalism may be traced to the frustrations with school of some learning-disabled youngsters.

The second major set of approaches to accounting for why students vandalize can be divided into general societal problems and specific institutional ones (Zeisel 1975). Underlying both frameworks is the assumption that human behavior is governed by knowable and measurable external stimuli. In this view, delinquents respond to outside forces, and the chore of an intervention is to alter these forces to change the behavior it generates.

The general societal approach to understanding vandalism in schools has a long and honored history. Its origins are found in the ecological studies of Burgess and Parks, research on urban environments by Short, theoretical treatises on social pathology and disorganization, the subcultural theories of Miller, and the opportunity theories of Cloward and Ohlin. The basic avenue for explaining delinquency in general and vandalism in particular is through the "ills of society." Zimbardo, for instance, described destructive behavior as the result of the "deindividuation" of people—that is, the product of a society grown too mobile, too big, too transient, and too undisciplined. Eric Erikson, one of the era's more popular analysts, found this approach congruent with his own: he has argued that much of the difficulty with growing up today rests in the ambiguity of modern society. The lack of consistency in societal mores form the basis for what he terms the "adolescent identity crisis." One of the difficulties with this general societal approach, however, is that it leads to as many frustrations as it explains. It is often so amorphous as to defy any attempts to turn its broad strokes into practical strategies for dealing with the problems it illuminates.

One of the more recent developments in theorizing about youth crime and vandalism involves the examination of specific institutional threads in the larger society's fabric. These societal components usually include analyses of schools, churches, the media, family, peers, and others. Much of chapter 2 in this book will be devoted to looking at specific elements within the schools that the research indicates may shape how vandalism is conducted. In general, popular-press attention has been devoted to hypothesizing the role of relevant curriculum, quality of teachers, classroom discipline, and rights and responsibilities. To date, the evidence on each of these factors does not show that any one of them creates vandalism but that all, in conjunction with the ways that the schools operate, appear to explain many of the dynamics behind property destruction. In addition, peer influences are suspected of providing a significant backdrop to the kinds of vandalizing acts committed. The research on the more distant factors of family, church, and media do not hold as much promise. Nowhere has strong evidence emerged that any of these variables alone provide the key to unlocking the mysteries underlying school vandalism.

Defining Vandalism

Although the term *vandalism* has had currency since the Dark Ages, modern researchers have been unable to agree on how to define, classify, and tally it. The closest thing to an official definition of vandalism is that offered by the Federal Bureau of Investigation (FBI) in its *Uniform Crime Reports* (1975): "the willful or malicious destruction, injury, disfigurement, or defacement of property without the consent of the owner or person having custody or control." This definition is probably the most widely accepted and used, but it is not free from controversy. In one of the first major federally funded studies of school violence, Marvin. (1976) criticized definitions of vandalism such as the FBI's as being too broad, covering everything from arson and window breaking to graffiti. And therein lies the core of the definitial fuss: the scope, intent, and costs of the destruction.

Much of the theoretical literature on school vandalism reflects the popularity of a broad approach to a definition, such as that offered by the FBI. Greenberg (1969), for instance, suggests a most inclusive definition: "acts that result in significant damage to schools." Goldmeier (1974) simply uses "destruction of property" to define vandalism, and Baughman's (1971) definition includes "all forms of property destruction, deliberate or not." Ducey (1976) has offered one of the broadest definitions in proposing that vandalism, as a symbolic attack on the school, include any destructive behavior ranging from littering to arson.

Narrower approaches to the term have arisen largely in studies and reports attempting to quantify destruction. Although not always agreeing on what to include under the vandalism category, studies estimating the scope of the problem done by Slaybaugh (1975), Grealy (1975c), the Baltimore City Public Schools (1974), and the National Institute of Education (*Safe School Study* 1977) have opted for tighter definitions.

Vandalism is also defined in the literature by its intent. This is an approach that is difficult to apply in practical terms, for few vandals are ever caught. Nevertheless, the intent of the destruction has been examined from a number of angles. Cohen categorizes vandalism on the basis of the significance it holds for the vandal (Shaw 1973) including:

acquisitive vandalism: damage done to acquire money or goods, for example, breaking into vending machines or phone booths.

tactical vandalism: damage done to attract attention or to advance some cause, for example, damaging the cafeteria to protest bad food

ideological vandalism: damage done to further some ideological cause, for example, bombing the U.S. Army recruiting booth in the school

vindictive vandalism: damage done for revenge, for example, stopping up urinals in retaliation for nonsmoking rules

play vandalism: damage done as part of a game, for example, jamming a telephone receiver in the most ingenious way

graffiti: damage done to express one's identity or some other message

malicious vandalism: damage done as part of some rage or frustration with the school

The recent *Safe School Study* (1977) has classified offenses against the school according to whether they were directed against school property—burglary, property destruction, or theft, for example—or whether the offenses were directed toward disrupting school routine—fires, bomb threats, or false alarms, for example. Thaw distinguishes among willful, careless, and thoughtless acts of damage, and Ducey conceives of it according to its pragmatic and symbolic intentions.

Another way of defining vandalism is by its costs. The traditional way involves dollars lost, but Blauvelt (1976) has added an important distinction between dollar costs and social costs. He divides dollar costs into high and low vandalism losses and social costs into similar high and low categories. High-social/high-financial-cost vandalism includes such major destruction as burning the school library, destroying school records, or other activities that could close a school. Low-financial/high-social-cost vandalism would encompass racial graffiti, destruction of minority group student projects, or killing classroom animals. Low-social/high-financial-cost vandalism might include large numbers of broken windows or damaged vending machines, and low-financial/low-social-costs would include such incidents as tire tracks on the school lawn and toilet paper in the trees. Blauvelt has further divided the social costs of vandalism into educational, psychological, and intergroup categories.

A final major classification scheme is provided by Zeisel (1976), who combines both cost and intent dimensions. He distinguishes between consciously and "not purposely" motivated vandalism and between vandalism requiring immediate and long-range attention by the schools. Consciously motivated vandalism requiring immediate attention is termed malicious. An accidentally broken window near a basketball goal would be classified as non-purposeful and needing immediate attention or "misnamed vandalism"—not vandalism at all. Consciously motivated damage requiring eventual attention is tagged as "non-malicious," and nonpurposeful vandalism needing eventual attention is conceived as "hidden maintenance" damage.

As part of this project, conducted under the auspices of the Council of the Great City Schools, nearly 1000 randomly selected school districts across the country were surveyed to identify promising programs. Questionnaires were eventually sent to 247 of the districts that indicated through a card or letter that they were operating a vandalism-prevention program. Of the 107 districts responding to the questionnaire, 67 percent identified themselves as urban, 28 percent as suburban, and 5 percent as rural. A literature review conducted for the project had uncovered fifteen offenses consistently mentioned under the vandalism rubric. Each of the districts was asked to indicate on a checklist which of the fifteen offenses and costs it included in its official vandalism tally.

Almost all districts responding to the questionnaire included property destruction and glass breakage in calculating their vandalism rates, yet there was tremendous variation in the reporting of such things as damage to automobiles, bombings and bomb threats, and graffiti. It is likely that some districts count categories like burglary and bomb offenses when adding up their vandalism losses while others handle them in a separate reporting category. Surprisingly, 24 percent of the districts indicated that they included mechanical or nondeliberate fires in calculating their vandalism rates. The following is a list of the 15 vandalism offenses and the percentage of responding districts that included each act in their vandalism tallies:

Offense	Percent
1. General property destruction	99
2. Glass breakage	99
3. Defacing property	89
4. Miscellaneous disappearance of property and equipment	88
5. Burglary	88
6. Theft or larceny	84
7. Breaking and entering	84
8. Arson	78
9. Graffiti	61
10. Deliberate damage to automobiles	44
11. Bombings or bomb threats	33
12. Fires of mechanical or nondeliberate nature	24
13. Littering	19
14. Loitering	9
15. Normal wear and tear	1

School districts were also asked to indicate whether or not the intent of property destruction was taken into account. Sixty-two percent of the responding districts reported that their estimates of property loss included only willful or malicious acts; no one stated that their estimates included only accidental damage; and 38 percent of the districts indicated that they included both accidental and malicious property destruction when estimating their vandalism losses.

We were also interested in knowing how financial costs of vandalism were computed in local school districts. When asked how they calculated their dollar losses, 6 percent of the responding districts indicated they included only those dollars that could be reclaimed from an insurance company. Thirty-one percent of the districts reported that their losses were calculated only on the basis of dollars that could not or were not currently being reclaimed from an insurance company. Sixty-three percent of the responding districts stated that their dollar costs were figured on the basis of both reclaimable and nonreclaimable losses. An interesting footnote to these figures is that a far greater proportion of suburban school districts than urban ones used both reclaimable and nonreclaimable costs to estimate vandalism losses. Furthermore, the distribution of school districts that did not or could not reclaim losses through an insurance company was skewed toward the urban areas. The importance of these figures becomes evident when trying to discern who suffers the greater amount of property loss, the urban districts or the suburban.

The sampled school districts were also asked to specify whether their vandalism rates were figured on the basis of financial losses, educational or social costs, or discrete incidents. Thirty-three percent of the responding districts reported that they used only dollars to describe their vandalism; 2 percent used only some measure of educational cost; and 6 percent used only discrete events. Most school districts used some combination of measures. Five percent of the districts included both financial and educational losses; 40 percent used financial losses and discrete events; another 14 percent included all three measures. The use of dollars to describe or calculate vandalism rates is clearly the most common measure.

Finally, school districts that used dollars to calculate their vandalism losses were asked to indicate exactly what financial costs they included. Ten percent of the responding districts included the costs of their annual insurance premiums; 45 percent included the costs associated with implementing or running a vandalism program; 55 percent included the costs of replacing or repairing damaged, defaced, or stolen property; and 12 percent included the costs of routine maintenance or repairs. Again, suburban school districts were more apt to include a wider variety of costs than were the urban districts.

The results of this survey should, of course, be treated cautiously and should be interpreted beyond those 107 districts only with some risk. But their descriptive characteristics have some use here. In general, contrary to the belief of some that districts underreport their losses, the survey suggests that many districts use a great deal of latitude in their reporting practices.

Approaches—Not Answers

This book was prepared for school administrators and researchers interested in reducing school vandalism. Experience has shown that many administrators, lacking solid information on program options, are likely to choose the most readily available solutions to their vandalism problem. The pressures growing out of the political climate or the seriousness of school damages may force administrators to choose the most highly visible and tangible response rather than the most appropriate one. After a school has been burned or a principal's office bombed, the local community may immediately turn to the superintendent or school board for a quick program to address the problem. Even minor damage, like that caused from graffiti, can bring harsh community reaction when the destruction is highly visible or has gone unrepaired over a period of time.

Unfortunately, the "quick fix" may cause more problems than it solves. In their final report, "Challenge for the Third Century: Education in a Safe Environment," the Senate Subcommittee to Investigate Juvenile Delinquency concludes:

> Approaches that advocate the quick cure and easy remedy will often fail because they ignore the complex and diverse causes of these problems. Meaningful progress in this area can only be achieved by engaging in sober assessment, not hysterical reaction and instituting thoughtful measures rather than making glib promises. From the beginning it has been the subcommittee's contention that a proper environment for learning is not merely the absence of violence and vandalism but is the presence of an atmosphere in which parents, teachers, students and administrators have the means to address the underlying problems which result in these eruptions (U.S. Congress 1977, p. 3).

Instead of providing pat formulas, we try in this work to describe, from programs already in existence, how board members and school administrators can go about the process of identifying the extent of their vandalism problem; selecting an appropriate set of administrative and programmatic strategies to attack it; involving students, teachers, support personnel, and the community in carrying them out; and appraising whether or not the effects of the program on vandalism are worth the fiscal and human costs.

To help in this process of program development, a wide range of potentially successful antivandalism strategies are described. Current program literature suggests, however, that the process of selection itself may be as important as what is chosen. Many have learned to their dismay that buying an attractive intrusion-control device or setting up a new human-relations program without a process of problem analysis and consultation causes as many long-term difficulties as it resolves. By focusing primarily on approaches, rather than quick-fix solutions, we hope to engage school managers and their many constituencies in a process that will lead to long-term vandalism reduction without sacrificing learning or the system's responsibility to its community.

This book is intended to address those temptations to adopt the nearest program by talking about ideas and strategies that work. Based on a comprehensive national review of effective and antivandalism efforts, and a thorough review of the relevant literature, it discusses what can be done, in school systems with differing populations and needs, to control and reduce vandalism. The book is intended to be used by school staff, teachers, superintendents, parents, students, and concerned citizens. We do not claim that the recommendations will eliminate vandalism in any setting, but we think they can help.

2

A Review of the Research

This chapter spells out, as briefly as possible, what is known about school vandalism and what remains to be learned, based on a review of the literature. Special consideration is given to the results of the congressionally mandated *Safe School Study* (1977) because of its high quality. It must be emphasized, however, that the findings presented here represent only national trends. It is essential that each school district assess carefully the nature of its own vandalism problem. More information on how to do such an assessment is contained in chapters 3, 4, and 5.

Extent of School Vandalism

Several attempts have been made to develop a nationwide picture of vandalism in the schools. The earliest study estimating the national cost of vandalism was conducted by the Office of Education (OE) in 1969 (Rubel 1977c). This study, which included both theft and arson in its vandalism figures, estimated that vandalism accounted for about $100 million in school property losses annually. A year later, the National Education Association (Rubel 1977c) calculated the losses to the schools at $200 million annually. This $200 million estimate was published in numerous articles and cited as official for a number of years.

Between 1972 and 1975 several other studies appeared that attempted to bring the national school vandalism picture into better focus. Furno and Wallace (1972a) estimated the national loss due to school vandalism at $150 million. The Education Research Service (1974) placed the national loss to be about $100 million (Rubel 1977c). On the basis of an informal phone survey of twenty- five school districts for Market Data Retrieval, Inc., Dukiet (1973) estimated the costs attributed to vandalism at $260 million and those associated with providing school security at an additional $240 million. The misleading combined estimate was later published in a nationally circulated news weekly (*U.S. News and World Report*) and formed the basis of a great deal of testimony before the 1975 Senate Subcommittee to Investigate Juvenile Delinquency (U.S. Congress 1975b). In 1975, The National Association of School Security Directors released survey findings that, when extrapolated, resulted in a national estimate of school crime cost at $549 million (Grealy 1975c). Later, others in the popular press rounded the figure to an even $600 million and applied it to losses due solely to vandalism.

The discrepancies in these estimates resulted, understandably, in a great deal of confusion (see table 2-1). Three studies were then undertaken: the American Institutes for Research (AIR) Study (Klaus 1977) commissioned by the Office of Juvenile Justice and Delinquency Prevention within the Law Enforcement Assistance Administration (LEAA); the National Center for Educational Statistics (NCES) survey; and the National Institute of Education (NIE) *Safe School Study* (1977). The AIR Study, which served as one piece of a larger effort to pool the resources of LEAA and the Office of Education estimated the annual costs of vandalism at $180 million. This estimate was made on the basis of data collected for the NCES portion of the congressionally mandated *Safe School Study* (1977). The NCES study consisted of a survey of crime reported to police between 1 September 1974 and 31 January 1975 in eight thousand

Table 2-1
Estimates of Costs of School Crime

Amount	Costs Included	Author	Year
$100 million	Theft and arson	U.S. Office of Education (OE) (Greenberg 1969)	1969
$200 million	Theft and arson	National Education Association (NEA) (Wells 1971)	1971
$150 million	Total national loss in schools	Furno and Wallace (1972a)	1972
$86 million	Total national loss in schools	Educational Research Service (ERS) (1974)	1973
$260 million & $240 million for school security	Crime and school security	Market Data Retrieval, Inc. (Dukiet 1973)	1973
$600 million	Vandalism	Popular Press (*U.S. News and World Report* 1974)	1974
$594 million	All school crime and security costs	National Association of School Security Directors (NASSD) (Grealy 1975c)	1975
$180 million	Vandalism and all crime and property destruction	American Institutes for Research (AIR) (Klaus 1977)	1977
$94 million	Offenses against the school (no arson)	National Institutes of Education (NIE) (*Safe School Study* 1977)	1977
$216 million	Offenses against the school	National Center for Educational Statistics (NCES) (*Safe School Study* 1977)	1977
$200 million	Best estimate of cost of property related offenses against the schools.	National Institutes of Education (*Safe School Study* 1977)	1977

schools in forty-eight hundred school districts. The results of this survey—which uncovered significant and expensive acts of arson—were extrapolated to give an estimate of about $216 million per year for all crime and property destruction, of which vandalism was only a part.

The NIE portion of the same study provides the best picture to date of the extent and nature of school-property destruction. The study indicated that the total cost of offenses against schools in a typical month was about $7.8 million or $94 million per annum. (The discrepancy between the $94 million and the $216 million estimate has been explained in part by the fact that the NIE survey included no acts of arson.) Approximately twenty-four thousand of the nation's eighty-four thousand schools report some vandalism each month, according to the *Safe School Study* findings (1977).

Given this, the authors of the *Safe School Study* (1977) conclude that the most accurate estimate of the annual costs arising from property related offenses against the school is about $200 million. Of this amount, about $40 million are due to vandalism alone and $60 million are accounted for by offenses like arson. Although involving heavy property losses, arson is not usually counted as vandalism per se.

Trends in School Vandalism:

The second part of the question on the extent of school vandalism involves trends in property destruction. Much of what is known of this aspect of vandalism must be gleaned from the literature on a district-by-district basis. Bellevue, Washington, for instance, reported losses of $1.35, $1.44, $2.11, and $3.03 per pupil for the 1970 through 1973 school years (U.S. Congress 1975a cited in Klaus 1977). Wichita, Kansas (U.S. Congress 1975a) reports that over the ten-year period between 1963 and 1973, the overall cost of vandalism jumped from $18,777 per year to $112,117. From a survey of 120 California school districts, Greenberg (1969) found that the total losses due to vandalism amounted to $1.7 million in 1965–1966 and to $3.0 million in 1967–1968. Studies by Slaybaugh (1973, 1974, 1975) also show that, except for 1975 when there was a decline, there has been an increase in the average dollar amount spent by school districts to fix damaged property. Data collected by Rubel (1977c) show, in addition, that between 1974 and 1976 the vandalism arrest rate for 15 to 17 year olds rose sharply.

There is other evidence, however, that suggests vandalism may be declining in severity or, at least, may be getting no worse. An examination of the surveys done between 1970 and 1974 by the Baltimore City Schools of thirty-one major urban school systems shows that eighteen systems experienced an increase in dollars lost to vandalism and thirteen declined or showed no change. The overall 10 percent rise in costs due to vandalism in those thirty-one cities was more than offset by the 30 percent increase in the consumer price index for urban workers during the same period. Watson (1976) has shown from data collected in Baltimore, Berkeley, Dade County, Detroit, Gary, and Los Angeles during the 1972 through 1975 school years that the overall trend in vandalism and other offenses is down. In an annual National Education Association poll, 11.4 percent of the sampled teachers reported having their property damaged by students in 1974; 8.9 percent of the responding teachers reported the same experience in 1976. Gold and Reimer (1975) conducted a number of surveys of adolescent self-reporting of property destruction and other offenses in 1967 and 1972. Their findings indicate that student participation in acts of vandalism declined over that period. In addition to these studies, the *Safe School Study* (1977) found from its survey of school principals that the percent of respondents claiming that vandalism was a serious problem remained about 8 or 9 percent from 1971 to 1975.

The research on the seriousness and trends of vandalism is by no means conclusive. Readings of identical data have elicited widely varying interpretations of the magnitude of the same problem. Dukiet (1973), for instance, claims that the losses due to property damage would equal the nation's annual textbook bill. Rubel (1977c) figures that the total loss in dollars amounts to only one-half of 1 percent of the total value of all school property in the country. The authors of the *Safe School Study* (1977) offer this tentative answer to the questions, "How bad is it?" and "Is it getting worse?": "It is worse than fifteen years ago but about the same as five years ago."

Targets of School Vandalism

The targets of destruction have been of particular interest, because they are likely to give the best clues as to why vandalism is occurring. One of the first studies in this area was conducted by Bradley (1967) of 232 school districts. Results of this study showed that 36 percent of the schools' losses were due to damages to lavatories, doors and walls, furniture, and the grounds; 21 percent were due to damaged textbooks; 19 percent to maintenance costs due to theft, breaking and entering, equipment damage, and glass breakage; 14 percent to instructional supplies; 7 percent to damaged library facilities; and the final 3 percent to miscellaneous damages.

Statistics kept by the National Fire Protection Association (1973) suggested that about 25 percent of all school fires originate in the classroom. In addition, Stretton (1977) found that the principal's office was the site of a large percent of major acts of vandalism. Two other important studies suggest that the school building per se is the most frequent target of destructive acts. A survey conducted by Slaybaugh (1975) indicated that the building itself was the most common target of vandalism, followed by the classroom, washroom, school bus, and cafeteria. These results need to be viewed cautiously; they are based on a questionable sampling method and a meager 15 percent response rate. However, similar results were found in the NCES portion of the *Safe School Study*. Of the total cost to repair or replace school property damaged due to crime, the NCES survey showed that 66 percent went for damages to the school's physical plant, 25 percent to equipment losses, and another 9 percent to supplies and book losses.

Nature of School Vandalism

Much of the work on the kinds of vandalism has been done only in the last five years. The first national study that attempted to describe the offenses being committed was done by Slaybaugh (1975). The results of this survey indicated that 39.6 cents of each dollar lost was due to fire damage, followed by 25.4 cents to glass breakage, 19.6 cents to property destruction, and 15.4 cents to equipment theft. Glass breakage was the single most common act of vandalism, and arson was the least, although the most expensive per incident. Close to 95 percent of all school districts responding to Slaybaugh's survey reported some glass breakage; only 36 percent of the districts reported any fire loss.

The *Safe School Study* (1977) was able to make estimates of the kinds of offenses being committed with much more confidence than the Slaybaugh (1975) study. Of the total 86, 593 property-related offenses committed in a typical month, NIE (*Safe School Study* 1977) estimates that 16 percent are due to trespassing, 12.7 percent for breaking and entering, 15.4 percent to theft of school property, 48.9 percent to property destruction, 5.7 percent to fires and false alarms, and 1.3 percent to bomb offenses. Surprisingly, many of these latter offenses are never reported to the police. Only 63 percent of the bomb offenses and 70 percent of the breaking-and-entering incidents are ever reported. The study also examined the number of schools reporting various kinds of vandalism. Of the nation's 84,834 schools, 10.9 percent report at least one incident of trespassing in a typical month, 10 percent report breaking and enterings, 12.3 percent report theft of school property, 28.5 percent report property destruction, 4.5 percent report fires or false alarms, and 1.1 percent report bomb incidents. Of these offenses the schools lose most per incident with burglary ($183) and the least with bomb offenses ($16), which are typically threats only.

The Vandals

The research on the characteristics of school vandals has, in general, followed the same line as the classic epidemiological studies of juvenile delinquency appearing from the 1920s to the 1940s. Despite its strong historical roots, research on the vandal has been largely unproductive; few consistent patterns have emerged. Early research depicted the juvenile vandal as a lower-class minority male with personality problems (Clinard and Wade 1958, and Bates 1962 cited in Zweig and Ducey 1976). Chilton (1967) has shown however that a large number of vandals come from middle-class backgrounds. Additional evidence for this finding can be seen in the high rates of property destruction in suburban schools. Goldmeier (1974) has found that vandals were, for the most part, white; Richards (1976) has shown that, in some instances—graffiti in particular—girls were as likely as boys to vandalize, and that the majority of vandals were 12 to 14 years old. Richards (1976) also demonstrated that students who reported having vandalized showed no greater incidence of psychological disorders than those who did not vandalize. In addition, Bartlett (1976) found that most vandalism occurred in a group setting.

Based on the delinquency literature, it has been hypothesized that student vandals were probably not performing well in school. Nowakowski (1966) had found that a high percentage of vandalism in secondary schools was caused by students who had been left back a grade. Ellison (1973) found that schools with high percentages of their students achieving below grade level also experienced high rates of vandalism. Greenberg et al. (1975) have shown that over 70 percent of the identified vandals he studied had a history of truancy and that 33 percent habitually cut classes. Yankelovich (1975) uncovered a positive relationship between students who had been suspended and the intentional destruction of property. Murillo (1977) also showed that a school's more alienated students were the ones most likely to vandalize. Richards (1976) demonstrated that students' daily interaction with authority figures correlated significantly with school vandalism. She concludes that student experiences with the school and its personnel and the activities of one's peers have the most dramatic impact on the decision to vandalize.

One of the few studies conducted that asked students about their own vandalism was done by Bartlett (1976). In this study 46 percent of the students admitted destroying property, but few perceived the behavior as criminal or malicious. Most saw their vandalism either as part of a game or as a means of retaliation at the school or a particular individual within the school.

The issue of intruder-as-vandal has received a great deal of attention in the literature. Testimony before the Senate Subcommittee on juvenile delinquency (U.S. Congress 1975b) indicated that up to one-fourth of all property-related offenses was caused by intruders. Other literature has suggested that school staff and even security personnel might be involved. The *Safe School Study* (1977) has found, however, that most property-related offenses (80 to 90 percent) were caused by students enrolled in the victimized school at the time of the incident. The study did show two exceptions: a large percentage of trespassing and breaking-and-entering incidents were committed by nonstudents.

One additional variable related to the family. As part of the *Safe School Study* (1977), students were asked to rate the level of discipline in their homes. The results showed a low but definite negative correlation between family discipline and the amount of school property loss. The correlations were higher for junior high schools than for senior high schools. In general, schools where parents participated in school activities and where parents exercised strong discipline over their children experienced less damage.

When Does the Destruction Occur?

Like crime in other segments of the society, the rate of vandalism in schools fluctuates tremendously depending on the hour, day, and month. A report by the National Fire Protection Association (1973) estimates that about 78 percent of all school fires occur after class hours and at least 45 percent of all such fires after 10 P.M. Similar results are seen in studies conducted by Leftwich (1977) and Anderson (1977). In addition, Bradley (1967) found that the bulk of all school vandalism occurs in the spring—a result contradicted by Leftwich (1977) who found the fall to be the worst time for senior high schools and the summer for elementary and junior high schools.

The *Safe School Study* (1977) provided an extremely detailed account of what offenses take place when and where. The findings indicate that offenses directed against school property occur most often on weekends, before and after school, and during vacation periods. About 98 percent of the breakins and 72 percent of all other property offenses happened when others were least likely to be around. On the other hand, offenses that were aimed at disrupting school routine were most likely to take place during the school day. From 62 percent to 73 percent of all false alarms, fires, and bomb threats occurred during regular school hours.

Additional analyses of the data show the relative risks to the school of experiencing a particular kind of offense during school, before and after school, and on the weekends. Schools are most likely to experience burglary on the weekend and theft, trespassing, property destruction, bomb incidents, and fire incidents during the school day. Those offenses that do happen after hours occur on the weekends, not before and after school. The exceptions are bomb and false-alarm incidents, which are most likely to take place before and after school—when they occur during nonschool hours. In addition to these trends, the data also show seasonal fluctuations: breakins and other property offenses tend to occur toward the end of each semester, especially in November and December.

Where Does the Destruction Occur?

The only major study to consider the location of the school as an aspect of vandalism was the *Safe School Study* (1977). It found that schools in the Northeast and in the West run a greater risk of property-related offenses than those in the North Central or Southern regions. This pattern was consistent across all property offenses except breaking and entering, which occurred in the South at an equal rate as that in the West. The findings were not quite as neat when one considered the urban, suburban, or rural location of the schools. Again, the study has divided offenses into those most likely to occur when others are absent and those that occur when others are present. For the former, results indicate that it is the large-city schools that run the highest risks of trespassing, breaking and entering, and theft of school property. Property destruction, however, is as high if not higher in the small cities and suburban areas. The differences in rates of disruptive acts, however, are not generally significant from one region to another. The NCES data confirm the notion that school vandalism is not unique to the urban schools. If anything, there is some tendency for suburban schools to experience greater dollar losses from vandalism than schools in other areas. Fifty-seven percent of the total national losses occur in suburban schools, despite the fact that suburban schools represent only 38 percent of all schools in the country.

The Schools

As vandalism became more prevalent in the 1960s, researchers began looking at characteristics of the schools that might account for some of the high rates of property destruction. The findings on these characteristics have been somewhat more consistent than information on other factors surrounding school vandalism.

The demographic characteristics of highly vandalized schools were the first variables researched. Work done several years ago by Slaybaugh (1975) indicates that the costs of vandalism were positively related to the size of the school district. Results of a survey conducted by the National Association of School Security Directors (1975) also showed that the number of burglaries was higher in the large school districts. Work by McPartland and McDill (1975 and 1977) and by Leftwich (1977) indicates that the size of the school may have more to do with serious disruptions than the size of the district or the size of the community.

Several studies have failed to link vandalism rates with the personal characteristics of school staff (Leftwich 1977 and Hamilton 1976). One study, however, uncovered a positive correlation between vandalism and the numbers of counselors in the schools (Debuzna 1974). Ducey has pointed out that the only schools that appear to be immune from extensive vandalism are small, private, affluent, highly academic schools and schools with considerable community involvement. Daniels (1976), Palmer (1975), and Ellison (1974) also showed that community involvement in a school has a positive influence on the reduction of property damage.

Although the findings by Slaybaugh (1975) indicated that large urban school systems suffer the lion's share of vandalism, other researchers have uncovered evidence suggesting the problem is as prevalent in the more affluent suburbs. Greenberg's (1975) study of school systems in California and Daniels (1976) study in Florida showed that vandalism losses do not correlate significantly with socioeconomic criteria. Gingery (1946) had discovered similar results two decades before. Goldman (1961) felt that the level of school vandalism had more to do with the transience of the local area. These finds were largely inconclusive, however, until the *Safe School Study* (1977).

As expected, the study did find that vandalism losses vary greatly according to the grade level of the school. In general, secondary schools experience greater damage and disruption than do elementary schools. There is some variance, however, within secondary schools. Senior high schools report more trespassing, theft of school property, and fires per month than do junior high schools. On the other hand, junior high schools report more breaking and entering and more general property destruction. One interesting finding of the *Safe School Study* was that a far greater number of incidents are required before secondary-school principals rate their schools as having a serious problem than are required for elementary principals. This is not terribly surprising given that some destruction, if not normative, is at least expected among secondary students.

The same study also found that vandalism rates were higher in large schools, in schools located in high-crime areas, in schools—especially senior high schools— where the students lived in close proximity to the campus, and in schools with a large number of nonstudents present during the day. It also noted that vandalism did not correlate with teacher-student ratios (which actually vary little from one school to another because of union and federal regulations), with the proportion of minority students in the school, or with the percentage of students whose parents are on welfare or are unemployed. The background variables of community crime level, geographic concentration of students, school size, nonstudent presence, and general family discipline account for approximately 19.5 percent of the total vandalism variance in urban junior high schools, 13.3 percent in urban senior highs, 17.8 percent in suburban junior highs, 9.3 percent in suburban senior highs, 39.8 percent in rural junior highs, and 22.1 percent in rural senior highs.

In addition to these basic demographic characteristics, a number of studies done prior to the *Safe School Study* looked at variables within the schools. Cohen (cited in Greenberg 1969), for instance, found that "the highest rates of school vandalism tend to occur in schools with obsolete facilities and equipment, low staff morale and high dissatisfaction and boredom among the students." Leftwich (1977) and Stretton (1977) also uncovered a relationship between vandalism and a high teacher-turnover rate. Goldman (1961) found in low-damaged schools that teacher-teacher and teacher-principal interactions were less formal; teachers had a higher degree of identification with the school; dropout rates were lower; and students were more interested in their work. Research by Pablant and Baxter (1975) and by Debuzna (1974) showed that low-damage schools often featured better upkeep, landscaping, and physical appearance.

The *Safe School Study* (1977) looked at many of these variables and others. In general, the study found that vandalism rates tended to be lower in schools where:

1. parents supported strong disciplinary policies
2. students valued their teachers' opinions of them
3. teachers did not express hostile or authoritarian attitudes toward students
4. students did not consider grades important and did not plan to go to college
5. teachers did not use grades as a disciplinary tool
6. teachers had informal, cooperative, and fair dealings with the principal
7. students did not consider leadership an important personal goal
8. schools whose rules were strictly enforced.

Moreover, it was also found that vandalism tended to be high in schools where personal violence was low. When internal school factors such as governance, faculty-administration coordination, student academic aspiration, school authoritarianism, and grade as a disciplinary device are considered alongside the demographic characteristics discussed, about 46 percent of the vandalism is accounted for in urban junior high schools; 28 percent in urban senior high schools; 22 percent in suburban senior high schools; 65 percent in rural junior high schools; and 42 percent in rural senior high schools.

What Do We Need to Know?

We have a much better notion now of the dynamics surrounding school vandalism than we had even two years ago. Further demographic and small-scale studies are still needed, however, to address the following areas.

1. Current data suggest that urban and suburban schools experience about the same amount of vandalism. The data, however, do not take into account the differing value of urban and suburban school property. We also need a better handle on the possibility that suburban schools may be reporting a wider range of acts of vandalism than urban schools.

2. At present we know that there is a correlation between school size and vandalism rates. Better data are needed to indicate which acts of vandalism increase as a function of school size.

3. Although there are reasonably good cross-sectional data on vandalism by grade level, we do not know how vandalism changes as students mature.

4. The various targets of vandalism offer one hope of understanding its dynamic. Yet we do not have adequate data on which targets are typically vandalized in urban and suburban schools and on which are damaged during what months of the year. Are the increases in vandalism at the end of each semester explained by increases in particular acts on particular targets, or is there an across-the-board increase?

5. A number of anecdotal reports indicate that the summer months may see the greatest share of school-property destruction. Better data are needed that indicate whether these impressions are true and to specify the profiles of vandalism during the summer. Are different kinds of acts committed against different targets and for different reasons?

6. The *Safe School Study* uncovered a moderate correlation between school vandalism and crime in the surrounding community. Additional studies are needed that specify which community crimes are correlated with which kinds of school vandalism. In addition, we need to know more about schools that actually witness decreases in vandalism while crime in the surrounding community increases.

7. Indirect clues in the literature suggest that vandals largely are disenfranchised at school. This is appealing from a common-sense point of view, but we need to know for sure. In addition, we need to know what makes some students vandalize and others not. Do those who do not vandalize vent their frustrations with the school or with individuals in the school some more acceptable way? Does the difference between vandals and nonvandals rest simply in their access to legitimate means of releasing frustrations? How does school vandalism relate to what is known about why humans become violent?

8. Much of the available research indicates that factors within the schools may account for the greatest share of property destruction. We have now only the scantiest knowledge of what those factors might be. Not much is known about how school disciplinary policies or individual teacher or counselor behaviors affect property-damage rates. In addition, not much is known about how daily interactions between students and school personnel influence damage. Small-scale studies designed to uncover some of these factors may be the most promising areas in which to conduct future work.

Summary

In this chapter, we discussed and compared the findings of recent research on school vandalism. Annual replacement and repair costs due to school property offenses are estimated at about $200 million, with wide divergence in the available data. Destruction of buildings and facilities causes the greatest dollar loss—the largest cost category appears to be replacement of broken glass.

Several studies suggest that student vandals, who commit 80 to 90 percent of all vandalizing acts, are more likely than others to be achieving below grade level, alienated from school, and more frequently suspended. In general, schools where parents participated in school activities and exercised strong discipline over their children experienced less damage.

Research about when and where vandalism occured showed few surprises: burglary on weekends; theft, trespassing, and property destruction during the day. Schools in the Northeast and West had higher vandalism rates than the rest of the country. Urban schools experienced more trespass, breaking and entering, and theft; small cities and suburbs had at least equal rates of property destruction.

A number of research studies have sought to correlate diverse variables with school vandalism. School size and district size have shown positive correlations with vandalism; on the other hand, community involvement appears linked to reduced property damage. The comprehensive *Safe School Study* (1977) found higher vandalism rates in larger schools, located in high-crime areas, where a large number of nonstudents are present during the day. In other studies, high vandalism correlated with high teacher turnover and low staff morale, and low vandalism rates correlated with schools that were well maintained and landscaped. The *Safe School Study* (1977) found that a large proportion of school vandalism could be explained by a combination of demographic and organizational variables, including discipline, student-teacher and teacher-principal relations, and expectations.

3 School Vandalism: An Analysis of Major Options

Not only does the research literature present a bewildering diversity of findings, but the experience of innumerable school districts has yielded a wide array of program strategies aimed at reducing vandalism. This chapter is devoted to summarizing the kinds of programs that school systems across the country are trying and to delineating some of the salient features of each.

A number of ways to categorize vandalism programs have been offered over the last few years, but one that appears particularly useful involves three broad headings: (1) environmental programs—programs that attempt to alter or protect the physical structure of the schools; (2) behavioral programs—programs that attempt to support, modify, or influence student behavior in school; and (3) system programs—programs that involve systemwide changes in the content or operation of the school. These three categories seem particularly helpful because they adequately separate programs by their focus. Environmental programs were aimed at the physical school facility itself; behavioral programs were aimed at students; and systemic ones were aimed at the institutional policies of schools. In the first broad category—environmental programs—three additional program types are identifiable:

1. Building security: programs using mechanical or electrical alarms, police or security personnel, student patrols, or some other kind of monitoring or detection procedure
2. Target hardening: projects that made it more difficult to destroy property, such as plexiglass windows
3. Architectural change: programs where the design of the building was changed or where the school was renovated or beautified

Within the second category—behavioral programs—are the following program types:

1. Offender accountability/responsibility: programs to detect troublesome students or outside offenders, removing them from the school premises or requiring them or their parents to replace or restore property or take part in special programs

---

The information for this chapter was gathered from the literature, a survey of over one thousand school systems, and from site visits to six particularly promising programs.

2. Behavioral change in students: programs using some form of incentive—usually money—to reduce vandalism
3. Human relations: programs that stress better intergroup relations, motivating group discussions, counseling, and student projects

Finally, within the third category of system programs, the following three program types have been identified:

1. Community relations: programs relying on the participation or involvement of the community
2. Institutional change: programs where the disciplinary, legal, organizational, or social structure of the school was changed to reduce disruption
3. Curriculum innovation: programs using new teaching material or courses

The remainder of this chapter is devoted to outlining the major features of each of these nine categories of programs. When evidence on program effectiveness is available, it has been included—but it must be admitted that evaluations and cost-benefit studies of various program strategies are almost totally nonexistent. Chapter 4 will provide additional information on how some of the programs described in this chapter operate in real school systems. A strategy for developing or updating a program is presented in chapter 5.

Building-Security Programs

The programs that appear most often in the literature involve building security. The NIE *Safe School Study* (1977) found that nearly half of the districts in the country used some kind of security measure to reduce both crime and vandalism. Nearly six of ten school districts surveyed as part of this work rated their security program as the most important part of their antivandalism effort. The main idea behind programs of this type is to watch or monitor school property and to identify vandals and intruders. The variation comes in who or what is doing the watching. A description of some of the more prominent watchers follows.

Silent Alarms

These systems, when tripped, sound an alarm not at the school but at some other location, custodian's office or the local police station, for example. They can be relatively simple to operate but can range tremendously in cost from one manufacturer to another. The *Safe School Study* estimated that about 18 percent of all schools use a system of this kind. Among the big cities, Cleveland, Norfolk, Portland and Washington, D.C., have tried these systems.

Highlights of Silent Alarms

Advantages:	Fast response time
	Will not alert vandal or intruder
Disadvantages:	Possible high installation costs
	High rate of false alarms

Local Alarms

Systems of this type use special lights, buzzers, or other noises to scare vandals or intruders out of a building and to alert security personnel. This traditional alarm system can be both simple and fairly low-cost for the average school building—depending on the company and area of the country. Almost all school districts in the country use some local alarm system.

Highlights of Local Alarms

Advantages:	Inexpensive to install and maintain
	Have long life
Disadvantages:	Assumes vandal will be intimidated by noise
	Relies on security personnel getting to scene faster than vandal can leave

---

Detection Alarms

Alarms of this kind borrow from the latest technological advances to identify and signal the presence of an intruder. Most of these systems can be found in big city school systems or in large suburban districts. The *Safe School Study* estimated that about 46 percent of all urban districts now rely on a system of this kind. There are now seven types of detection alarm systems available:

1. Microwave detectors transmit a high-frequency beam, which, when acti-

vated, trips an alarm. Colorado Springs, Colorado, uses this type of system. They report some success in detecting burglars.

2. Ultrasonic detectors have a shorter range than a microwave system. Generally they are most cost-effective. Grand Rapids, Michigan, and Hasbrough Heights, New Jersey, currently use ultrasonic devices with some success. Despite its cost effectiveness, the system can be periodically activated by air conditioners, moving curtains, and hanging plants.

3. Passive infrared detectors have been suggested as the least likely to experience false alarms. They sense heat and trip an alarm when a warm body passes within its field and have been specifically developed for small rooms. They are about as expensive as the ultrasonics. Fairfield, Connecticut, uses infrareds with some success.

4. Audio detectors are the cheapest of all detection devices and involve a receiver hooked into the school's public address system. Placentia, California; East Islip, New York; and New Orleans, Louisiana, currently use some form of audio detector.

5. Mechanical detectors are normally the least sophisticated and often the least reliable; they include devices attached to windows or doors to alert a monitor to some illegal entry. Newark, New Jersey, and Baltimore, Maryland, have experimented with them with mixed success.

6. Closed-circuit television, unlike the other systems, is designed to monitor behavior both during and after school hours. It can be the most sophisticated of all systems. Depending on the particular unit, it can enable one person to monitor an entire building. The system requires installing television cameras around the school and can be among the most expensive systems to purchase. The NIE reports that only about 3 percent of all schools use such a system. Most closed-circuit-television systems are located in the junior and senior high schools of large cities. New York, Alexandria, Virginia, and Texarkana, Texas, are using this kind of detector.

7. Personal alarms work like sophisticated walkie-talkies. They are usually hand-held and allow the person to signal a central monitoring station from anywhere in the building in case of emergency. There are a few systems that can be built into teachers' desks for classroom problems. Although only about 4 percent of all schools use these devices, they are found in nearly 40 percent of the nation's big city high schools (*Safe School Study* 1977). New York and Sacramento are using versions of this system.

Highlights of the Detection Alarms

Advantages: Useful in protecting property after hours
                          Can be used to monitor outdoor areas
                          Often highly effective
                          Can be used to protect people

Fast response times
Usually manpower effective
High variation in number and types of systems
available

Disadvantages: Usually expensive to install and/or maintain
Sometimes difficult to adapt to physical characteristics
of given building
Can result in high rate of false alarms
Involve only small number of people in operation
May present prison-like appearance
Require constant monitoring

To date, there is little hard evidence to demonstrate the effectiveness of any of these hardware systems. Most of the major studies in this field have focused on the prevalence of vandalism rather than the effectiveness of the various security devices. A few have examined property losses before and after installation of a particular system in a single school district, therefore producing results of fairly low quality and limited generalizability. The *Safe School Study,* however, was able to survey school principals on their perceptions of the effectiveness of these systems. In general, principals rated these devices as their most successful tool in reducing overall school crime. Reported least reliable by the principals as a security measure were the portable personal alarm systems. Among the most reliable were closed-circuit televisions, security vaults, and a variety of small protective devices (which will be discussed later in this chapter). On the whole, security systems are perceived to be highly effective in reducing after-hours property damage. Most schools report reduced vandalism costs no matter which of these systems they are using.

Most experts agree that if night vandalism, burglary, and intrusions have gotten out of hand, an automatic hardware system can help. The trick is in choosing one. The experience of a well-qualified building engineer would be invaluable at this point. There are a number of things one should look for when considering any of these systems (Vestermark and Blauvelt 1978), including:

1. Whether the hardware is rated by Underwriters Laboratories, The State Insurance Fire Rating Bureau, and The Factory Mutual Engineering and Factory Insurance Association. (See *Vandalism and Violence: Innovative Strategies Reduce Costs to School* in appendix A.)
2. The guarantee for performance of the system in your particular school. (See *Controlling Crime in the School* in appendix A.)
3. The exact nature of what the equipment is supposed to do in your school buildings. (See appendix A.)
4. The recommendations of other school systems using the equipment you are

considering. (Look back through the systems we mentioned here as using a particular kind of hardware.)

5. The degree of maintenance required—Ask for repair records of systems installed by the company elsewhere. (See appendix A.)
6. Length of time needed to get spare parts or to repair equipment when broken (Coursen 1975).
7. Normal false alarm rate (Coursen 1975; see appendix A).
8. Price of equipment, completely installed (see appendix A). (Ask if dealer is willing to install system into single school on a test basis.)
9. History of company in installing such security equipment in other school districts (see appendix A).
10. Length of time the equipment has been on the market (see appendix A).
11. Necessity of training program to run the system.
12. Behavior necessary to baffle or defeat the system under consideration (see appendix A).
13. Visibility of system and its likelihood to attract vandalism.

Although this chapter summarizes the major points of these systems, one may want to look through appendix A (section on Building Security, Design and Target Hardening) to see if other materials are attractive. In addition, chapter 4 describes a district that has successfully implemented a major hardware system.

Security Personnel

Security systems of this genre rely less on sophisticated hardware to monitor school grounds than on professional or paraprofessional security personnel. The *Safe School Study* estimated that about 7 percent of all schools across the country are using security forces. This percentage is deceptively low in that more than one-third of all big-city schools employ trained security personnel; more than 50 percent of all urban junior high schools have such personnel, as do two-thirds of all big-city high schools. In fact, the study reports that about 20 percent of all city secondary schools use uniformed police officers. About 5 percent of the large urban schools use police stationed inside school buildings, and 11 percent report having police stationed around the school grounds.

The use of regular school staff to monitor property loss and other crimes is also common. NIE reports that about 76 percent of all schools in its sample designated an administrator to be responsible for security and discipline. Nearly 85 percent of the urban schools used this kind of system, suggesting a more organizationally distinct function for security in these districts. In addition, many schools reported using their custodial personnel for some security duties. This practice was not as common in the urban schools (21 percent) as it was in small cities (30 percent) or suburban areas (25 percent).

Highlights of Using Security Personnel

Advantages: Quick response time
                 Usually dependable
                 Presence discourages destruction
                 Allows flexibility of assignment
                 Often rated as effective
                 Can use CETA funds to pay salaries

Disadvantages: Can be very expensive without additional funds
                 Expensive to train or keep trained
                 Can present repressive appearance
                 Dismissal of incompetent people difficult

The skills, duties, and characteristics of school-security personnel have been particularly troublesome to pinpoint. Part of the difficulty involves the variety of personnel used. In general, three broad categories of security staff include local police, contract guards, and school-security professionals. A recent survey by the Education Policy Research Institute (EPRI) of 56 large school districts showed that the duties of all these groups range from general patrol activities to instructing and counseling students. The same survey, however, found that little to no special educational training was provided to handle these duties. The training and supervisory aspects of using security personnel are probably the weakest parts of a system like this. EPRI has found in its survey that police activities in the schools go virtually unmonitored.

The evaluative data on the use of security personnel also are not particularly good. The *Safe School Study* was unable to uncover any direct connection between the presence of security personnel and low property destruction; however, many of the principals in the study rated security forces as successful in reducing overall crime rates. In addition, the principals surveyed as a part of the *Safe School Study* rated security personnel as highly dependable, more dependable in fact than most security devices. Only 1 percent to 3 percent of the principals rated personnel as not dependable, as opposed to a 17 percent undependable rating for electronic-detection systems. There is even less evidence to point clearly to which kind of security personnel to employ, although there are many things about each to be considered.

Although the use of local police is common—especially in the urban secondary schools—a number of factors should be considered before employing them. Many school systems use police not only for straight security duties but for counseling and other educational tasks. "Officer Friendly" and other community relations programs have attracted a degree of acceptability in school systems across the nation. Use of the police in driver education, drug abuse classes, civics classes, and various group sessions with students has raised problems in some systems when the officers begin to see their traditional police duties as being diluted. Vestermark and Blauvelt (1978, p. 65, 67) have suggested that to overcome problems of this nature it is advisable to draw up a contract with the police force specifying:

1. number of police officers to be assigned in and around the schools
2. wage rate (often on an hourly basis) and whether these wages cover extra-curricular activities, such as dances and football games
3. whether the officers on duty will be uniformed and/or armed
4. whether the same police personnel will be assigned to the same school each time and whether they will be "on duty"
5. channels through which complaints can be made about specific officers and how unsatisfactory officers can be removed from duty
6. the nature of training to be provided to the officers (See appendix A.)
7. the role of the principal of the schools where the police are assigned
8. police access to student records for investigative purposes
9. review procedures for periodically assessing police effectiveness

---

Highlights of Police Personnel
(Vestermark and Blauvelt 1978, pp. 66, 67)

Advantages: Highly trained
                   Flexibility in force size
                   Clearcut reporting procedures
                   High-visibility deterrence
                   High authority in community
                   High commitment to job

Disadvantages: Answerable to both schools and police force
                   Usually armed and uniformed
                   High school-assignment turnover
                   Privacy problems and student resentment
                   Costly

The use of contract security forces is a second personnel option for schools. It is often considered less desirable, however, because accountability is lower. Not uncommon is the practice of employing the security force that has offered the lowest bid for services. These forces can present an effective deterrent to destruction in the schools and can act as a stop-gap measure while recruiting other personnel, but their long-term effectiveness remains suspect (Vestermark and Blauvelt 1978).

> *Highlights of Contract Personnel*
> (Vestermark and Blauvelt 1978, pp. 67, 68)
>
> Advantages: Low cost
>   Flexibility in force size
>   Greater discretion in building-level assignments
>   Greater right of board to fire unsatisfactory personnel
>   Greater discretion in how personnel will dress
>
> Disadvantages: Often poorly trained personnel
>   Low commitment to schools
>   Presence may stir student resentment and disrespect
>   High guard turnover
>   Poor supervision

School districts across the nation are using some interesting variations with their forces, both contract and administrative. Memphis and Nashville, for instance, have tried using guard dogs to protect school property after hours. Antioch, Illinois, is using male and female security personnel to protect its school district. Oklahoma City and Decatur, Georgia, are using their custodial and maintenance staffs to patrol and protect school property. (These custodial programs have received particularly high marks in the literature for efficiency and cost effectiveness.) The local police in Buffalo had instituted a special pawn-shop detail to recover stolen school property. Flint, Michigan, is using lay personnel to patrol the schools; Lakewood, Colorado, has hired an all-female security force; Lauderdale Lakes, Florida, has actually moved its police station into a middle school; and Scanborn, New York, has deputized some of its school staff. One city is even using its local volunteer civil-defense force to watch over the schools.

Again, there is not much evidence to indicate which security personnel systems are more effective. Training and commitment are generally higher among contract guards and security professionals. Principals surveyed as part of the *Safe School Study* (1977) rated police put on regular patrol around the schools as least dependable for security purposes, but police in the school buildings, contract security guards, and custodians were given higher ratings. School-security professionals were rated as most dependable among the groups mentioned. Vestermark and Blauvelt (1978, p. 71) suggest that most schools may want to consider a mix of security personnel, indicating that full-time school-security professionals may be preferable for long-term work with school staff and students, police for short-term high-visibility duties, and contract guards for routine patrol assignments.

Community Security

Of growing popularity are programs that include the community in fighting vandalism. Community security programs usually take two forms: asking neighbors
to watch the school after hours and moving families into homes on school
grounds. New York City and Houston have systems relying on persons living
near the schools to watch over school property. Mesa, Arizona, has asked local
citizen-band operators to watch for and report acts of vandalism. All use the
same approach: parents and neighbors watch the schools for intruders and call
the police if they observe anything suspicious. The *Safe School Study* found
that elementary schools were more likely than most to make use of parents
for security purposes, since parents hold greater authority for younger children.

Programs where families are moved onto school grounds are also becoming
more prevalent. These kinds of programs are especially common in small towns
and suburban areas. The program works something like this: the district moves
or builds a mobile home on school grounds; a family moves into the home rent
and utility free; the homes are hooked into a school alarm system; and the
residents call the police in case of trouble. Mesa, Arizona, and Jacksonville,
Florida, are two systems currently making use of this kind of system.

In both types of programs, the biggest problem involves the selection of
reliable parents or residents. It is usually wise to prepare a written contract
for trailer residents specifying responsibilities, vacation time, and liabilities.
Many school systems have reported finding trailer watch residents among their
custodians, school staff, graduate students, or police and other law enforcement
personnel.

Highlights of Community Security Personnel

Advantages: Extremely low cost
                   Involves parents and other local residents
                   Improves sense of community
                   Moderately effective

Disadvantages: Less control over parent security teams
                   May be less reliable
                   High rates of false phone calls

Evidence on effectiveness is again sparse. The *Safe School Study* (1977)
found that principals rated parent monitors, guards, or watchers as more dependable than any other kind of security personnel. Few districts have relied

heavily on this kind of system as their chief security device, however. Nashville, in fact, has found that neighborhood school-watchers have a tendency for calling the police after spotting night watchmen or custodians on school grounds. There is little evidence to suggest a strong link between neighborhood school-watchers and any lowering of school-property damage. Still, the idea has some advantages in terms of intangible benefits and might well be used to supplement other security systems.

Trailer-watch programs deserve higher marks. They appear to be both cost efficient and effective. Most school systems using trailers report decreases in burglaries and other property-related offenses after an initial outlay of about $15,000 per trailer. This is the kind of program, however, that grows more expensive each year with the rising costs of mobile homes and utilities. There is little to suggest that these programs outperform hardware systems, but their cost-effectiveness gives them a substantial edge over the more sophisticated technology. (See chapter 4.)

Student Patrols

Using students to police school grounds is also becoming very popular and is receiving a great deal of praise from local-level administrators. The *Safe School Study* (1977) found that the use of students to patrol the schools was third in popularity in the big cities only to the use of school security professionals and contract guards. Nearly 26 percent of the big-city schools have students monitoring school grounds, as opposed to 16 percent of smaller city schools, 11 percent of suburban schools, and 7 percent of rural schools.

Some of the best-known student-security programs are found in Pittsburgh, Pennsylvania, Prince George's County, Maryland, and Oahu, Hawaii. Oahu, for instance, has a volunteer "Juvenile Patrol" roving school grounds during the weekends. The programs in Pittsburgh and Prince George's County involve student relations as well as building security. In Prince George's County, student council members and other volunteers form a "security advisory council." The Council advises the school on student problems and hosts a number of school activities each year. Members of the Council also patrol parking lots, monitor locker rooms, man rumor-control centers, and act as homeroom spokesmen. This program is receiving a great deal of national attention, along with positive responses from students.

The Pittsburgh program has many of the same features, except that its "Vandalism Patrol" is in operation only during the summer months. In addition, patrol members are paid by the district for their security services. A unique feature of the program is that its participants are in many cases students who have been caught vandalizing. Officials cite the leadership abilities of the members as the salient characteristic of the effort.

Highlights of Student Patrols

Advantages: Inexpensive to operate; can use federal CETA dollars
Involve students in school security
Build sense of responsibility in students
Thought to be effective in reducing damage

Disadvantages: Require participants who are respected by other students
Participants require some training
Possible legal problems if a participant is injured

Evidence supporting the effectiveness of student patrols is a problem. Most school systems using students to monitor school grounds also use a variety of other measures, making it difficult to tell how much the patrols contributed to the reduction in vandalism and burglaries. Program officials in Pittsburgh and Prince George's County report that the programs are easy (and actually fun) to run and that they have seen a marked reduction in property thefts, larcenies, and other property-related offenses. The *Safe School Study* (1977) found that principals rated student patrols as dependable as parent patrols, both of which received higher ratings for reliability than the police, janitors, contract guards, and school-security personnel. Despite the lack of hard evidence on these kinds of programs, they do have intangible positive side effects for students and school officials, and therefore deserve serious consideration by most school systems.

To have a student program that is effective, a number of factors need to be considered. Many educators and parents see this kind of program as totally inappropriate for students. This is a legitimate opinion; students should not be forced to participate in the program. On the other hand, there are measures that can be taken to lessen the fears of parents (Vestermark and Blauvelt 1978). Things to be considered include:

1. involvement of parents in the planning and running of the program
2. role of the school-security personnel in supervising student patrols
3. age group of students participating in the program
4. types of incidents participants are likely to encounter
5. leadership abilities of the program participants
6. student training
7. roles student participants will have in suggesting school-policy changes or enforcing security regulations
8. manner in which program participants will be selected

The most important part of a program like this involves training. Vestermark and Blauvelt (1978) suggest that program training should accomplish three things: it should expose students to the realistic situations they would likely face on duty; it should provide students with enough skill and confidence to perform their security tasks; and it should build the group into a cohesive security team. Specifically, the training segment of the program should teach participants (1) personal confidence and teamwork, (2) techniques of conflict reduction, (3) how to coordinate their work with security personnel and/or police, (4) how to use security hardware, like alarm systems or walkie-talkies, and (5) pride in their work. Parents and school staff should be kept informed at all times as to the progress of the program, including its failings. For a detailed description of how to use students in a school-security program, see Vestermark and Blauvelt, *Controlling Crime in the School* (listed in appendix A of this work).

Protective Devices

School districts across the country are also using a myriad of security techniques in addition to those mentioned. Although hardware systems are designed to detect intrusion and personnel systems to monitor school grounds, we have used this category of protective devices to refer to techniques designed to limit access to the schools. Programs designed to make it difficult to destroy and to gain advantage from acquiring school property are included in the next section on target hardening.

The most common protective devices in use today include special procedures for handling school keys, outside locks, security vaults, difficult-to-scale fencing, special identification cards, hall passes, visitor policies, and signs. Data gathered through the *Safe School Study* indicate that nearly all schools in the country make use of some protective measures to limit access to school facilities. Nearly half of all big-city schools now use special locks on their outside doors to restrict access. In addition, most school systems now have policies concerning visitors to school buildings. NIE has found that about 6 percent of large-city schools now require students to carry a special identification card; 41 percent require students to carry a hall pass when out of class; and 67 percent require visitors to check in at the main office.

Highlights of Protective Devices

Advantages: Relatively low cost
                Moderately effective
                Low maintenance costs
                Little training needed to operate

Disadvantages:	Devices can be beaten by ingenious students
	Present repressive appearance
	May cause student resentment

Most districts using building-protective devices report moderate success. It is difficult to know for sure how many thefts, burglaries, and acts of vandalism are foiled because of a locked door. It is reasonable to assume, however, that these devices will probably pay for themselves in property saved. As the only method used to protect school property, they leave much to be desired. As a supplemental security system, their worth appears more defensible. It is important to consider the possible negative effects of these efforts, also. Children locked out of the school building after the first bell, and the appearance of identification cards, do little to strengthen confidence in schooling. When implementing them, it may be worthwhile to design them to be as unobtrusive as possible. Moreover, clear policies should be developed for granting access to keys, especially those to rooms where high-cost educational equipment is kept.

Target-Hardening Programs

Target-hardening programs attempt to make the school less physically vulnerable to damage and therefore are on the front line of the preventive process. The programs also include those that try to make it less attractive to abscond with school property. There are a number of target-hardening strategies being tested across the country, the more common of which involve the installation of break-proof windows, special lighting, and specially marked school property.

Lighting school grounds during the evenings is a particularly common security measure. The *School Product News* survey (Slaybaugh 1973) reported that 42 percent of school districts used special lighting techniques for security. Syracuse, Dallas, and Baltimore are all school systems that use flood lights or other lighting devices to ward off vandals. San Antonio has used the opposite approach and is now turning off all lights at night. The district is reporting not only a significant decrease in vandalism but also a saving in energy costs. There is little evidence, however, that lighting alone is an effective deterrent to vandals.

Marking school equipment or recording serial numbers is also gaining popularity in many areas of the country. Programs of this type are normally administered by local police authorities and are designed for schools, business, and residences. School systems in Tulsa and Minneapolis use this technique to keep track of equipment. The FBI reports that programs like these make thieves less likely to steal property, although hard evidence is not available.

The installation of break-proof windows is probably the most common target-hardening measure. The *Safe School Study* (1977) found that nearly 70 percent of the large urban schools used unbreakable or plastic windows to cut property loss. Other districts report significantly less of this than the urban districts. Lexan, polycarbonate, and fiberglass are frequently used as materials for windows, all of which are more expensive than glass. Baltimore and Minneapolis have been using these windows for some time, reporting mixed success. Although their use can reduce the recurrence of broken windows, they can be melted with propane lighters. Because glass breakage is the most common and among the most expensive forms of vandalism there seems to be some merit in using break-proof windows. The cost of installing them is small compared to the cost of continuously replacing broken glass. Many suggest that break-proof materials be installed a little at a time to hold down the costs to schools.

Other target-hardening techniques include fastening desks to the floors, keeping school grounds free of gravel, installing break-proof student lockers, removing cash and other valuables from the schools in the evenings, and even moving bathroom sinks into the hallways.

Highlights of Target-Hardening	
Advantages:	Essentially preventive in nature
	Many low-cost measures
	Require no training
	Moderately effective
Disadvantages:	May present appearance of repression
	Not always dependable

In addition to the types of target-hardening techniques just discussed, there are literally dozens of other measures a school can take in preventing destruction. One of the better tools designed to make a school's property less prone to damage involves a checklist developed by Zeisel (1976). It offers suggestions on how to harden or redesign play areas, doorways, walls, parking lots, buses, gyms, and fixed hardware to reduce property loss.

There is not much convincing data, however, to show that these techniques work. The *Safe School Study* (1977) indicates that about 8 percent of the surveyed principals rated unbreakable windows as undependable. Although good data are not available, common sense would indicate that many target-hardening measures hold promise for reducing some deliberate damage and much accidental destruction.

Architectural-Design Programs

These programs involve altering the physical structure or appearance of a school to lessen property damage. Genuine architectural efforts aimed at reducing vandalism are rare, especially in school systems unable or unlikely to build new buildings. Most school systems are experiencing declining enrollments and have little need to build new school facilities. Still, some districts are continuing to build and may want to consider architectural efforts at reducing vandalism and/ or options for their existing structures.

Several schools across the country are being redesigned architecturally to reduce both accidental and deliberate property damage. Broward County, Florida, and Portland, Oregon, are two districts that have tried this approach with existing buildings. Using grants from the Law Enforcement Assistance Administration (LEAA), these districts modified a number of schools using Oscar Newman's concept of "defensible space." The basic idea is to design space within a building so that the natural flow of people encourages their watching the premises. The concept has been repeatedly tested with some success in experimental-housing units in cities.

Highlights of Architectural Programs

Advantages:	Addresses basic design problems that encourage vandalism
	Usually unobtrusive in comfortable surroundings
	Requires little unusual or costly long-term care
Disadvantages:	Large initial outlay of funds
	Limited options for existing buildings
	Requires specially trained architects

Conclusive evidence is not in yet on the effectiveness of these efforts, but preliminary results indicate that vandalism and other crimes can be markedly reduced by architectural programs. Architectural programs may require massive doses of money and expertise and are clearly beyond the capabilities of most school districts. For administrators unable to restructure their schools, general target-hardening techniques may help. In addition, one may want to consider simple building alterations like windowless doors and "graffiti walls." Should remodeling a school be an option, make sure that the design allows for easy surveillance and that materials can be easily cleaned and are not breakable.

We have also categorized school beautification efforts under this heading because they involve changing the appearance of the schools to discourage property damage. The rationale behind school beautification is that students and others will care better for their school and will have more pride in it if it looks nice. Louisville and Mesa, Arizona, are two districts having some success with these efforts. Louisville has run a beautification project with identified vandals and "troublemakers." In Mesa, students are encouraged to paint murals on the walls and decorate the hallways. Districts in San Bruno Park, California, and Warren, Michigan, give awards to students and schools showing particular pride and neat appearance.

Programs designed to beautify and build school pride have shown mixed results. They apparently work well in elementary schools and among students who tend to be involved in the life of the school anyway. There is always the possibility that when schools are competing with each other for prizes, students from one school may act to subvert those from another. The positive aspect of these programs, however, is that they encourage students, school staff, and community to work together with a common aim. This fact, alone, makes these programs worth considering.

Offender-Accountability Programs

These programs are designed around the simple assumption that students should be held accountable for their behavior. They usually take one of two approaches: in the first, high-risk or troublesome students are identified by their schools and are diverted from the usual school program; in the second, students identified as vandals are required to repay the school for damages they have caused.

The first approach, the diverting of students, is very popular in school districts across the country. About 35 percent of the urban schools surveyed in the *Safe School Study* (1977) report transferring disruptive children to another regular school in the district, 10 percent report assigning disruptive students to special classes within the school, 10 percent report transferring such children to special schools for disruptive kids, and 40 percent report referring disruptive children to community-mental-health facilities. Programs of this nature usually involve the use of specially trained teachers and counselors working with students on an individual basis. The curriculum and work materials are normally changed, and the pace of study is fitted to the individual needs of the student. There are so many programs in operation that it is difficult to draw any conclusions about them. In general, they are designed not only to quell vandalism but to address a host of behavioral and academic problems.

The Youth Related Property Crime Reduction Program in Albuquerque is a good example of a vandalism-related-diversion project. The project uses police and school staff to provide remedial services to youth having a "high crime rate potential." Los Angeles is also testing several programs that use special educational or community services for "crime-prone" youth. The federally-sponsored cities-in-schools programs in Atlanta, the District of Columbia, Oakland, and New York City are set up in much the same way in that they attempt to identify high-risk children and provide a range of well-coordinated city services to them.

Highlights of Diversion Programs

Advantages: Meet individual student needs
                     Can bring several services to bear on child

Disadvantages: Can be expensive to run
                     May label child as delinquent or worse
                     Require well-trained, highly motivated staff

---

The second form of offender program involves restitution for damages from identified vandals or their parents. The general theme of the programs is that identified vandals are charged for some of or all the repair costs. There are some variations in this approach. In Fresno, for example, vandals are taken to small claims court for restitution; Oklahoma City has implemented a policy requiring identified vandals to work off their vandalism debts. Most of these programs are accompanied by a vigorous attempt on the part of the schools or the local PTA to inform parents that they will be held financially accountable for damages caused at school by their children.

Highlights of Restitution Programs

Advantages: Hold students accountable for action
                     Regain some of vandalism losses

Disadvantages: Usually not cost effective
                     Difficult to administer
                     Present some legal problems
                     Apply only to students caught vandalizing

---

Unfortunately, there are several problems with these programs. Cost-effectiveness is problematic in that restitution rates are usually low, and the costs of running the programs can be high. Districts must pay the cost of identifying vandals, investigating incidents, preparing a case, and sometimes supervising student work. It is rare that schools ever identify more than 30 percent of their vandals (Zeisel 1976), and most school districts report restitution rates of no more than 4 percent of the costs of damaged property. In fact, there is some evidence to indicate that districts without parental-liability statutes have higher restitution rates than districts that have them (Furno and Wallace 1972b). There may also be legal problems with restitution efforts in states where a dollar limit is placed on the liability of parents for their children's damage. Moreover, in areas where a school district may settle claims out of court, there may be problems with the denial of due process. (For a discussion of additional legal problems see chapter 5).

A third kind of student-accountability measure involves simple discipline. Little more than expecting or teaching standards of acceptable behavior is involved here. Although a number of discipline centers or behavior clinics providing counseling and other personal services have appeared across the country (Rubel 1977a), schools rely for the most part on the same disciplinary tools they have always used. Data collected through the *Safe School Study* (1977) indicate that suspension and expulsion are still the most common disciplinary techniques. About one-third of all schools responding to the *Study's* survey report that they suspend students each month. The practice is somewhat more prevalent in the big cities, although suburban elementary schools report as many suspensions as those in the city. Similar patterns emerge with expulsions and paddling. Only a minority of school districts use student courts, although a recent inhouse survey by the Council of the Great City Schools indicate that all its members have student-rights codes in effect.

Unfortunately, the relationship between discipline practices and school vandalism is not well known. There is, however, no evidence whatsoever to support the notion that increased suspensions or expulsions will decrease property destruction or any other kind of crime. What has been shown repeatedly is that a fairly enforced policy of student behavior can contribute to student trust and to orderly schools. No other conclusion stands out so boldly as this in the dozens of studies done on school vandalism. (See chapter 5 for the development of such a policy and appendix A for resources on school discipline.)

Behavioral-Change Programs

These programs involve incentives to students for acceptable conduct and are based on the tenets of basic behavioral theory. Mentioned earlier were programs that reward students or schools for school pride, but the programs included in this category are oriented strictly toward the alteration of student behavior.

Here, the desired behavior is that students not damage the building, and the reward is often provided in terms of money. The programs included in this category are often termed "vandalism accounts."

It is difficult to know for sure how many districts use programs of this type, but they are growing in popularity. Oakland, California; White Plains, New York; and Shrewsbury, Massachusetts, are a few school districts experimenting with student-vandalism accounts. The way these programs work is that schools or student councils are allocated a certain amount of money by their central district office. From this fund all vandalism repairs are made, and any money left over goes to the students. There are some variations in who handles the money. In White Plains, N.Y., the administration is responsible for keeping tabs on the fund; students were allowed to decide how the money is spent. In Shrewsbury, on the other hand, students take responsibility for controlling the money—including paying vandalism bills.

Highlights of Student-Account Programs	
Advantages:	Reported to be successful
	Low or no additional cost
	Uses peer pressure to its best advantage
	Teaches responsibility
Disadvantages:	Requires staff time to administer
	May raise false expectations among students
	Possible to subvert the program by disinterested students or rival student groups

Districts trying this method report success; money is being returned to student councils in increasing amounts. Oakland, for instance, has seen its total costs of vandalism drop from $433,205 in 1977 to $133,306 in 1978. In addition the costs of running these programs are negligible. Despite their reported successes, there are inherent drawbacks. Rubel (1977a) has pointed out that: vandalism is not always caused by students attending the damaged schools; if no money is returned, student expectations for a reward are falsely raised; a small number of students not associated with the student council can subvert the program and run up enormous vandalism bills. Little evidence exists, however, that these problems are widespread, suggesting that the programs are worthy of examination.

A number of other programs exist that use more classic methods of modifying behavior. Colver and Richter (1971) have described the use of "behavioral contracting" to increase school attendance, respect for school rules and for grades and to decrease vandalism, smoking, and general disruption. The authors report a great deal of success, but it is always difficult to know how to enforce the contracts or what to do after they are broken. There are a large number of programs using these techniques; however, traditional behavior-modification programs fall outside the borders of this book. Nevertheless resources are included in appendix A.

Human-Relations Programs

This is a broad heading containing a number of types of programs aimed at improving interpersonal or intergroup relations or at increasing personal adjustment. Only rarely do programs of this nature focus on problems of property destruction.

The most common human-relations program involves counseling. Much of the counseling is done in individual or group settings, focusing on a number of personal and interpersonal problems and using a variety of counselors. The group doing the counseling is a distinguishing feature of most counseling efforts. Guidance counselors often are not the ones called on to deal with troublesome or problem students. The survey conducted as part of the preparation for this text indicated that counselors were rarely used in the designing or running of vandalism-reduction programs.

Over the last several years, schools have relied increasingly on "crisis counselors" to deal with problem students. Crisis counselors often are young adults with special training in such areas as community relations, parenting, social work, drugs and alcohol, and the law. They are, presumably, able to identify with those students whom most everyone else had given up on. San Jose, California; Philadelphia, Pennsylvania; and Los Angeles, California; are some of the communities using crisis counselors. Counseling in these programs involves both regularly scheduled meetings and impromptu dropin sessions. Although the evidence is scanty that counseling programs are effective on a wide scale, crisis-counseling programs receive high marks in the literature for turning around individual problem students. San Jose, for instance, is reporting particularly positive results.

Several districts employ police or security guards to counsel students. Roseville, Michigan; Meridian, Idaho; Lincoln, Nebraska; Santa Ana, California; and Sanborn, New York; are examples of communities using police counselors. From the literature, it appears that counseling is targeted on different issues depending on the counselor. The programs using a crisis counselor focused more on problems such as drug use, truancy, family troubles, and other personal difficulties, and programs using police counselors were directed to student crime, individual rights, involvement with the law, and the courts.

School districts such as Sunnyvale, California, have students counsel each other. These programs may involve counseling to resolve personal or family problems and are distinguished from traditional student-counseling projects only in the emphasis placed on the law, probation, and the courts. Student-to-student programs report as much success as those using professional counselors. The research evidence has, for some time, pointed to the fact that students are more likely to seek out each other for guidance than they are other school staff. Resources for designing peer-counseling and peer-tutoring programs are included in appendix A.

Approaches other than counseling are being used in some schools. Examples of innovative human-relations methods can be found in Wautosa, Wisconsin; Los Angeles, California; Omaha, Nebraska; New Rochelle, New York; and Oakland, New Jersey. In Oakland, for instance, students film the effect of vandalism on their school and show it to other students in assemblies. New Rochelle is using posters, slide shows, and buttons to build enthusiasm for its Project SAVE—Students Against Vandalism Everywhere. Students in Los Angeles's Vandalism Reduction Project stage plays (using a character called Vince Vandal), hold group discussions, and throw dances. Wautosa is showing a film called "Vandalism – Why?" to its students and holding group discussions. This and other films can be found listed in the Resource Guide.

Highlights of Human-Relations Programs
Advantages: Involves students in problem solving Humanitarian Inexpensive Targeted on troubled students
Disadvantages: Only indirect effect on vandalism Effectiveness not well demonstrated Requires highly motivated staff

There are few data on the impact of human-relations programs, in general, and counseling programs, in particular. Klaus (1977) points out that these efforts alone should not be expected to dramatically influence vandalism or violence rates. He goes on to argue, however, that counseling programs can be endorsed as a tool for making the school more responsive to the needs of students. Many who have described these programs in the literature point to positive side-effects such as improved student-police relations, higher attendance, better grades, fewer fights, and better-adjusted students. Although counseling by itself will not provide a final answer to vandalism, it points in the right direction.

Community-Relations Programs

The programs included in this category seek the involvement of parents, community groups, and neighbors in the life of the schools as a means of reducing vandalism. They differ from the community-building-security efforts discussed earlier in that these actively seek community participation in and use of school facilities.

Although the use of community programs addressed at school vandalism is low, there are some interesting projects around. New Orleans and Lawndale, California, for example, hold community forums and meetings to inform the public about the vandalism problem in the schools. Several districts are taking a more active approach. Louisville, Kentucky; Flint, Michigan; Los Angeles, California; Oakridge, Tennessee; and Torrance, California; are striving to develop a community sense of ownership in the schools. Torrance, for instance, has instituted an open-door policy for community members. In Flint and Oakridge, the schools are left open in the evenings for community use (see chapter 4). Both these districts are reporting good results in reducing property destruction and in improving attitudes toward the schools.

Highlights of Community-Relations Programs

Advantages: Builds community confidence in schools
                Moderately effective with night vandalism
                Builds on local resources
                Increases community involvement in the schools
                Low cost

Disadvantages: Program can be subverted by disenfranchised people
                Possible that program may attract vandals

Plans to open schools to community use have received much publicity in the literature. There are two assumptions behind this approach: first, the community will develop a greater sense of ownership in the school and will be more likely to protect it; second, vandalism—especially night vandalism— will be curbed by the presence of people in the buildings after hours. Despite the fact that Flint and Oakridge are reporting positive results, other school administrators are not finding the same degree of success with their programs. Olson and Carpenter (1971), in fact, found that vandalism increased with the number of hours the buildings were left open. It has been suggested that before programs of this kind are tried, a careful assessment should be done of the resource needs and the characteristics of the community.

Other districts are building their programs with a more active effort toward community outreach (see chapter 4). One of the most active community efforts found in the literature was the Cortez Street School Project in Los Angeles. The project in this school involved community luncheons, teacher walks through the community, parent participation in classes, an open-door policy, and a neighborhood block program. Other districts, like Warren, Michigan, are building community participation into their school-beautification projects. As with other programs, there is no clear evidence to indicate how successful community efforts are at reducing vandalism. Usually the projects require little money—only time and motivation—to implement. The enthusiasm with which they are described in the literature leads one to believe that, even if their impact on vandalism is indirect, they have enough positive side-effects to make them worthwhile.

Institutional-Change Programs

The programs under this heading are usually more comprehensive and policy oriented than the human-relations projects, emphasizing changes in the disciplinary, legal, organizational, and social structure of the school as an institution. The assumption behind these efforts is that the inequalities and unresponsiveness of policies and practices in the schools foster violence and vandalism. Remedies under this approach lead not to increased counseling and training but to restructuring the way schools conduct their business on a day-to-day basis.

Examples of institutional change programs can be found in Louisville, Kentucky; Chicago, Illinois; and Portland, Oregon. In Louisville, the Roosevelt School reorganized its policies to permit the participation of neighbors and parents in hiring, teaching, and curriculum. Chicago's Manierre School underwent a complete overhaul: new lines of authority, disciplinary policies, academic standards, and hiring practices were implemented. In Portland's John Adams High School, the entire school was divided into eight separate minischools, each using a different curriculum.

Other efforts have included the establishment of community-operated alternative schools. There are now several thousand alternative schools in operation across the country, and although most were not started to reduce vandalism, they experience very little of it. Scribner (cited in Berger 1974) claims that in the ten-thousand-auxiliary-student system in New York there have been no reports of violence or serious vandalism. The alternative schools set up for disruptive youth are usually not the Summerhill-type schools founded in the 1960s; but they employ dedicated staff, individualized academic and vocational programming, and flexible policies to achieve results. More information on alternative schools is found in the Resource Guide.

As was indicated in chapter 2, a number of pieces of research (*Safe School Study* 1977, McPartland and McDill 1977, and Polk and Schafer 1972) have suggested that the flavor and tone of school life at the building level (for example, school disciplinary policies, emphases on grades, teaching quality, principal's leadership, and grading) contribute significantly to how appealing students find vandalism.

	Highlights of Institutional Programs
Advantages:	Aim at underlying causes of vandalism
	Possible to obtain high commitment and participation
	Potential of possible results
Disadvantages:	Conceptually difficult to design
	Possible political problems in garnering support
	Need for highly motivated staff

Programs of the institutional type are invariably started for reasons other than curbing vandalism. Consequently, judging their effect on vandalism is difficult. The new schools that undertake such dramatic changes report positive results in other areas such as school work, grades, and student relations. The programs can also be difficult to implement; they often require outside technical assistance and well-motivated and resourceful administrators.

Curriculum-Innovation Programs

A number of school districts are testing new curricular packages, courses, and teaching materials to alleviate problems of crime. There is reason to believe that few of these projects are targeted at vandalism problems per se. An approach that is growing rapidly in popularity is general "law-in-education" courses, where students are taught about their responsibilities as citizens and the workings of the judicial system. The assumption here is that a knowledgable student is less prone to break the law. The verdict is still out on such endeavors; little is known about their ultimate effectiveness (Appendix A has a number of resources for those interested.)

A second approach that we found to be very creative and contemporary had been tested in Chesterfield, Missouri. There, a curriculum had been developed to create in students a better understanding of the vandalism problem. The approach used was ecological: students studied the problem of vandalism from an environmental perspective. In St. Louis, one school has built part of its mathematics course around the study of vandalism. The idea is to get students to realize the financial costs associated with property destruction.

Some schools are seeking to reduce the vandalism and violence within their walls by using new curriculum materials oriented to students' rights and responsibilities. Most of the rights-and-responsibilities packages are not directed toward school vandalism, however. For this reason, we have excluded them from this review; nevertheless, there are excellent packages available for the interested reader. The Constitutional Rights Foundation, Los Angeles, California; The National Organization on Legal Problems of Education, Topeka, Kansas; The National School Public Relations Association, Arlington, Virginia; The Center for Law and Education, Cambridge, Massachusetts; Phi Delta Kappa, Bloomington, Indiana; and the Institute for Political and Legal Education, Pilman, New Jersey, have all published curriculum guides on students' rights and responsibilities. Information on where and how to obtain them is found in the Resource Guide (see section on Rights and Responsibilities).

As was mentioned previously, many school districts are designing new materials and courses for students who have been removed from regular coursework. By and large, the bulk of these efforts involve remedial classes in the basic academic skills, supplemented with vocational, career, and technical training. Work-study courses appear to be an increasingly popular method for reaching disruptive or alienated students. Some research now indicates that there is a connection between inadequate vocational development in students and school crime (Cavan and Ferdinand 1975, cited in Klaus 1977).

Highlights of Curricular Programs

Advantages:	Involves teachers in solving problems
	Delineates lines of rights and responsibilities
	Teaches about effect of vandalism
Disadvantages:	Can be costly and/or time consuming to design materials

---

The success of these curriculum approaches in reducing vandalism is generally unknown. Some curriculum packages can be expensive to buy or produce, implement, and test. It should be stated, however, that the continued scrutiny of curricula for relevance to students can only be viewed as a good thing.

Summary

Chapter 3 focused on programmatic options available to school districts for dealing with vandalism. Nine program categories were discussed, divided into three broad groupings: environmental, behavioral, and system programs.

Building-security programs, which are the most common security measures in schools, received extended discussion. Seven program alternatives were analyzed, ranging from alarm systems to security and student patrols. Advantages and disadvantages of each system were cited, and relevant programs described. Target hardening and various architectural-design alternatives were presented as other environmental program options to be considered.

Three kinds of behavioral programs were described. Offender-accountability programs stressed making vandals responsible for their actions, through swift apprehension and restitution of damaged property. Behavior-change programs offered incentives to students to control vandalism through student accounts and other means. Human-relations programs were aimed at improving interpersonal or intergroup relations or personal adjustment, with reduced vandalism as an ancillary goal.

System programs stressed various aspects of organizational participation and change. Community-relations programs sought to involve parents, community groups, and neighbors in the life of the school, and institutional-change programs emphasized changes in the disciplinary, legal, organizational, and social structure of the school setting. Curriculum-innovation programs developed and tested new curricular packages, courses, and teaching materials aimed at understanding and addressing problems of school crime.

The chapter points out that evaluation results for most of the described programs are at best sketchy and inconclusive. Combined approaches directed toward the specific needs of individual schools and districts are therefore recommended.

4 Case Studies of Prevention Programs

In this chapter, a closer look is taken at programs in six school districts throughout the nation. The districts were selected because they represented different program types, geographic locations, and sizes. Each city was visited by one of the authors. The districts chosen include: Fresno County, California; Flint, Michigan; Madison, Wisconsin; Dallas, Texas; Alexandria, Virginia; and Escambia County, Florida. The programs in these districts represent attempts to restrict the amounts of school vandalism and efforts to lessen other kinds of community crime. Although general, the descriptions that follow provide a broad sweep of how school districts have marshalled their resources to stop school destruction.

Each program description focuses on the following components:

1. Creation of the program—an examination of the critical factors in establishing each program—is the portion of the study that looked at the overall nature, design, and scope of the particular program. Included were questions about the system's needs assessment, operational goals and objectives, and assumptions. Also taken into consideration were important political and economic factors in the early stages, including major sources of operating funds.

2. Operation of the program—the focus here was the actual functioning of the program, both in terms of how the program was put into place and how it was maintaining itself. Of particular concern to the authors were the specific implementation and maintenance aspects of each program; general staffing; community and city input into the program; use of resources; decision making; obstacles to the program (press, union, startup time, size of schools); and relationship of the program to police, city hall, and other groups. Also, to the extent possible, the authors tried to gain some sense of the dynamics surrounding these key findings.

3. Impact of the program—the final component concentrated on the major effects of each of the respective programs. Important in this regard were factors involving program usefulness and benefits to schools and community. The authors also examined, when appropriate, any new problems the selected approach may have created. Lastly, this section highlights any special accomplishments, results, or developments that might be interesting or helpful to others.

Fresno County, California

The location of this school system is in a mid-sized city located within a larger district in north central California. There are twelve high-school districts within Fresno County with an enrollment of 82,700. The type of program utilized was one of institutional change, and the contact person was William J. Bischoff, education/probation liaison.

Creation of the Program

Noting the need for coordination between the juvenile courts and the schools, Fresno County, California, has developed a program aimed at reshaping existing areawide resources for the prevention of juvenile delinquency and vandalism. Fresno County, like many counties across the United States, has begun examining ways in which existing youth serving programs could provide more comprehensive services in preventing acts such as vandalism. In Fresno County, to reduce delinquency and vandalism, new preventive efforts were developed among existing agencies. The program's overall goal was to promote cooperation between law enforcement, justice, and school personnel.

The program addresses the conflict and competition that arises among youth-serving agencies at the local level. By reassembling and creating new organizational structures, Fresno County has found it can plan and deliver better preventive services to juveniles. In September of 1974, the County of Fresno created a position of education/probation liaison (EPL), paid 50 percent by the schools and 50 percent by the justice system, to serve as a coordinating agent between the two institutions.

There were two factors present in the Fresno County creation of the EPL. First, the Fresno setting helped contribute indirectly to the creation of the EPL. Fresno is a medium-sized city surrounded by a large county with several small suburban and rural towns. There are twelve high-school districts within Fresno County, each with its own superintendent and seven high-school districts in the City of Fresno. In addition, Fresno Unified has a separate superintendent, and the larger association of county districts also has a superintendent of county schools, an elected position. The function of the county superintendent's office is to provide services, as needed, to the school districts (for example, audio-visual programs; educational television; and special consultant services in various academic areas). The EPL is housed administratively at the county seat and mandated to assist in providing services to the relevant county and city agencies. Its creation was facilitated by the geographic spread of the area and the visible need for coordination of resources.

The second factor that indirectly prompted the creation and maintenance of the position is California State Assembly Bill 3121, which takes status offenses by juveniles out of the juvenile court system and assigns them to local SARBs (school attendance review boards). SARBs include school-administration, teacher, parent/community, and social-agency representation, and require and use outside assistance for programs. There are currently eleven SARBs in the Fresno County system, and the EPL is just one of their resources.

Operation of the Program

The role of the EPL has been that of advocate, educator, coordinator, and planner, engaged in negotiating solutions in situations in which any agency impinges on another. The EPL coordinates an interagency advisory committee comprised of three subcommittees and multiple task forces with representatives from virtually every government agency and school authority serving youth at the local level.

The purposes of the advisory groups include: improving communications, coordination, and cooperation between agencies and decision makers; providing a forum for clarifying perceptions and expectations among agencies; identifying gaps and overlapping services; and addressing new and critical interagency issues as they are identified.

Other functions of the EPL include linking the Probation Department to the schools to provide a course on "Youth and Law," focusing on the complexity of the justice system and the consequences for youth who enter into it. The Education Department provided the equipment and materials for the Probation Department to develop a multimedia package to accompany the program.

In addition, the EPL has created workshops for administration and on-line staff in the justice system and in the county school districts. With facilitators from other fields, workshops were structured to build communication and discuss constraints on formal roles. Specific issues arose around probation, intake policies, court reviews of school attendance, and the confidentiality of records. Each issue was clarified in writing.

The EPL keeps a daily log of requests, which is used for a monthly report to the superintendent of county schools and the chief probation officer. The report is then used for long-range planning.

Impact of the Program

Local representatives spoke highly of the impact of the program. The program cost little to implement, but because of its administrative authority and priority it has had a significant effect in reallocating existing resources. It is believed that because of an improved youth-service program in Fresno County, crime and vandalism particularly targeted at the school were reduced.

The significance of the Fresno model lies in the fact that the school system has attempted to bring together a broad range of institutional resources to address its problems of school vandalism. It has chosen to view the problem at a more fundamental level by first focusing on the numerous services, facilities, and personnel currently working with Fresno youth. Through this approach, the overriding goal has become the better coordination of resources to maximize delivery of youth services. Even though the long-range impact of this ambitious, institutional approach cannot fully be measured at this time, the early results in Fresno County have nonetheless been encouraging.

Flint, Michigan

The Flint school system is in a primarily urban industrial district in central Michigan, seventy miles north of Detroit. There are forty elementary schools and thirteen secondary schools and an enrollment of 38,000 students and 1,900 teachers. A community-relations/building-security program is utilized— the community-school concept was pioneered in Flint almost forty years ago.

Creation of the Program

Flint was the birthplace of community education some forty years ago. With grants from the Charles Stewart Mott Foundation, Flint has pioneered the development of schools as neighborhood resources and the city itself as an open arena for educational opportunities. Flint recognized in the early 1970s that unless it took decisive action to change the direction of its schools it would soon be overwhelmed by a range of social and economic problems. With grants totaling almost $5 million a year from the Mott Foundation, the city made a concerted effort to test approaches to urban education involving the whole community.

Community involvement in the schools has had a significant impact on school vandalism, which is not perceived as a major problem in Flint. Individuals interviewed claimed this to be a function of the preventive model established citywide. That is, vandalism has been headed off through a variety of community-involvement measures, including programs that have influenced behaviors as well as attitudes of school staff and community residents. The worth of this approach was documented by the *Safe School Study* (1977), which identified schools where parents participated in school activities and supported school disciplinary policies as showing lower rates of vandalism.

Operation of the Program

Vital to the community-involvement philosophy are School-Community Advisory Councils comprised of parents, other residents, students, teachers, and representatives of many economic and social groups, including PTA, block clubs, civic groups, churches, and businesses. Each school has its own council and determines its own size. Generally, a council ranges between fifteen and thirty members. Secondary-school councils are elected; representatives may be appointed to the elementary-school councils. The councils study local problems and needs and plan strategies to solve them. The councils can examine any neighborhood or social problem they choose and have been known to take action in areas of crime and vandalism, curricula, human relations, planning and renovating school facilities, use of buildings, student rights, housing, drug abuse, traffic safety, and unemployment. The School Department also provides some inservice-staff assistance to these groups. All councils have input to the Board of Education as well as to their own citywide Advisory Committee. Each School-Community Advisory Council's chairperson is a member of the Citywide Advisory Committee, with an additional six representatives appointed from the community at large. The Citywide Committee meets with the Board each term to present its concerns and requests.

In addition, the superintendent and staff have created a formal Superintendent's Committee comprised of major agencies and institutions serving Flint. They meet regularly with the central administration to discuss mutual problems and concerns.

The involvement of the community has done much to head off vandalism, particularly during school and early evening hours (when the buildings are generally in use). The Flint Community Schools, however, have also relied in recent years upon a security system to protect the buildings overnight. A centralized Sonitrol System monitors the schools throughout the city and indicates through silent alarms when a building has been unlawfully entered. To date, maintenance staff working with the Flint Police Department have successfully apprehended or frightened off many unwelcome night visitors.

Impact of the Program

Through community involvement, school vandalism in Flint is confronted simply as one aspect of much broader community problems, such as high youth unemployment. This link between the community and the school regarding both problems and solutions was a strong point of reference for almost everyone with whom we talked.

A wealth of written information and experience exists in Flint around issues of community participation in reduction of crime and school vandalism. It is strongly recommended that districts interested in community education approaches contact the Flint Public Schools, Division of Public Information and Communication.

Madison, Wisconsin

Wisconsin's capital city is essentially an urban community surrounded by farmland. Its school system consists of thirty elementary schools, ten middle schools, and four high schools and has an enrollment of 30,000 students and 1,700 teachers. The type of program utilized is one of curriculum development and behavioral change in students. The contact person is Glen Borland, principal, LaFollette High School.

Creation of the Program

The Madison Metropolitan School System has developed three independent approaches to dealing with its vandalism problem. The first approach is a decentralized, autonomous planning process throughout the district to encourage local decision making and reduce the management size of the district. Substantial autonomy is given to the area directors in each of the four districts—particularly in vandalism prevention. Within each of the four districts, a localized approach is being taken to combat problems of vandalism. Ideas are exchanged regularly across districts, but all four area directors (who act as assistant superintendents) are free to pursue their own programmatic/curricular/ innovative approaches.

The second approach to solving vandalism problems is a program to foster interagency cooperation and coordination. As an outgrowth of vandalism in the schools and neighborhoods and an increased awareness of the lack of coordination of youth services citywide, the mayor's office and the local press were beginning to voice concern over the problems of vandalism. In 1975 an Ad Hoc Vandalism Committee was set up to examine both the causes and the solutions to the problem, with reports provided directly to the Common Council of Madison. Two other ad hoc advisory committees were created about the same time by the School Board to initiate coordination between the school and community. The two groups were: the Social Agency Coordinating Committee and the Business and Education Coordinating Council. Both these groups had districtwide membership and were designated to discuss a variety of issues, including vandalism.

The third approach involves a series of inschool curricular programs. A group of students, teachers, and custodians participated in a week-long workshop in 1977 sponsored by the Law Enforcement Assistance Administration (LEAA) on peer counseling as an approach to dealings with vandalism. At the time of our visit, the group had just come back with the outline of an "action plan" that included such elements as a student-service center, a media/public-relations component, and an inschool administrator's workshop. The enthusiasm from the one school which participated was also influencing other schools to implement programs.

Operation of the Program

A review of the operation of each of the three approaches follows.

A Decentralized, Autonomous Planning Process throughout the District. To effectively operate a decentralized system, staff need training and assistance in implementing programs. In response, a training and resource center was created called the "Exchange". A number of people in Madison were interested in a course offering entitled "Dealing with Vandalism," and interested teachers could opt to teach or simply study this topic for credit through the exchange. The center has been well used and has provided an administrative mechanism for practical building-level initiatives for staff who have become frustrated with daytime vandalism.

A Program to Foster Interagency Cooperation and Coordination. In 1978, the Mayor's Office created through official resolution a Youth Problems Committee. Results and activities of this group, as well as for the Ad Hoc Vandalism Committee, were not complete at the time this review went to press.

A Series of Inschool Curricular Activities. At the school level a number of efforts are being made by students (with the support of some adult staff). For example, one high school is piloting a cross-age, volunteer program in which a handful of high-school students working with volunteer teachers from some of the feeder elementary schools have developed a model, multimedia, role-play, open-conversation approach to explaining vandalism to the younger students. The program had some effect last year despite numerous problems (no credit for students; limited teacher support; overcommitment by active students; no exploration of why vandalism occurs; and so on.)

Impact of the Program

The impact of each of the three approaches has been positive, although no firm evaluation data have been generated. Due to the increasing financial strain felt by the Madison Metropolitan School System at the time of our visit, serious questions were raised about the school system's ability to maintain and operate the "Exchange" program, let alone evaluate its impact. At this time no data exist on the effectiveness of the program. The problem in Madison was similar to many other districts, where there was a lack of consistent data on vandalism and no uniform reporting criteria at a building level.

So far, the activities of these various committees set up to foster interagency cooperation have met with only limited success. One of the early difficulties involved the failure to include the police in the various ad hoc groups. The police had established their own low-key school-liaison program where officers met at least once a month with the area superintendent, the building (high school only) principal, counselors, and interested students to discuss issues of concern and to make recommendations and referrals. Unlike an earlier attempt that failed, the police do not deal with problems of discipline or control.

A final component of the program that has some potential for success involves the schools' informal links with the local university. One professor at the University of Wisconsin has been examining and coding all available school data on vandalism from the past five years (that is, looking at environmental factors, such as floor plans, size, location, and kinds of materials, and correlating them with the frequency of vandalism). Efforts are underway to field test program strategies and to interview high-school students, including some who have vandalized.

It will be some time before the impact of the array of inschool curricular programs can be evaluated. But, for now, the idea of developing a variety of approaches has a core group of adults and students interested and involved at one high school in particular and increasingly at others.

One aspect of this component that has had considerable positive impact has been the involvement and support of the school custodial staff. Their inclusion from the very beginning has helped build important cooperation between all the key groups within the school building. It has also allowed this often overlooked resource to establish a more active than reactive role with regard to vandalism.

Dallas, Texas

Dallas is one of the nation's major metropolitan centers. Its school district includes 135 elementary schools, 41 secondary schools, 6 magnet schools, and 26 others, and it has a total student population of 136,547. The Dallas system used an institutional-change/human-relations program to combat vandalism, and its contact person is Marvin Fleetwood, teacher-in-charge.

Creation of the Program

Almost ten years ago in Dallas, Texas, the general superintendent of schools, the county juvenile probation judge, and the chief of police met to discuss ways in which they could work together to address the growing problems of truancy and school security. The result of this top-level initiative was the establishment of a pilot Youth Action Center (YAC) within a junior high school severely troubled by truancy and juvenile crime. Since the success of that pilot effort, centers have been established in all twenty-one Dallas high schools to serve that building and its feeder schools.

The YAC model evolved, primarily, as a response to the problems that the three youth-serving agencies faced in dealing with truants in a city as large as Dallas. Prior to the establishment of the centers, juvenile officers who were legally responsible for truants had two options in dealing with a student found out of school. The student could be apprehended and taken to police head-quarters, a trip that could keep the officer out of his district for most of the day, or the student could be returned directly to school, where busy staff might or might not have the time and skills to deal with the problem.

Operation of the Program

Each YAC, located on school grounds and staffed by a teacher-in-charge, a police patrolman, and a juvenile-probation officer, provides a setting in which the three discrete agencies collaborate in managing truancy and related problems. The YAC model serves to clarify the responsibility of each agency in the enforcement of the truancy laws in Texas, while providing, in the same place, the skills and resources necessary to resolve many of the student's problems contributing to truancy. The team approach of the youth-serving professionals provides a range of services that can be coordinated appropriately for each student. For example, supervision may range from informal attendance checks by the teacher-in-charge to formal meetings with a county probation officer. Referrals come not only from police but also from principals, parents, and a variety of other agencies and individuals. Parents are contacted in approximately one-half of the cases, often through a home visit by both the teacher-in-charge and the police officer.

Services provided by the YAC extended to a variety of areas. The YAC staff locate jobs for youth, arrange medical care, locate day-care facilities for preschool siblings, make referrals for special education, coordinate the services of other community, social, and family agencies, and even provide shoes and clothing. YAC staff do act as liaison between the student and the principal, although there is now systematic interaction between staff and individual teachers.

The many diverse and successful services of the YAC, however, have only begun to address the multiple problems of vandalism. Due to the scope of the problem, Dallas found it necessary about five years ago to install security hardware as well as hire some uniformed security personnel. Over time, both services have been increased. Given the size and sprawl of the city, most night security is the responsibility of personnel in radio-equipped vehicles. These security people are in direct contact with their school-department supervisor as well as the police. The largest facility in the system, the massive Skyline High School, is protected not only by a YAC and patrol cars, but also by an internal-security force (on motor scooters) and a sophisticated alarm system. Although all security personnel have experience or training in security work, both the director of Security and the school system's own investigator are educators by training.

The YAC staff, through contacts with parents, a local advisory committee, and a variety of other public-relations efforts within each neighborhood, have also carefully built credibility within their districts. Neighborhood residents will often report suspicious individuals or events to the YAC, providing information that can prevent vandalism or assist in identifying vandals. This credibility is particularly vital in those areas of the city where there is intense suspicion and hostility to regular police officers.

Impact of the Program

One of the obvious measures of the success of the YAC model is the decline of neighborhood vandalism in the daytime. With the establishment of a YAC it has declined by as much as 37 percent.

The impact of the YACs has, however, been consistently broader than first envisioned. Although the presence of a uniformed officer within a school brought considerable resistance initially, school administrators are now convinced that the continuous presence of a security team has had a series of beneficial side effects. In fact, having a police officer on the grounds has reduced other crimes from speeding to drug sales. Furthermore, the YAC team members are both known and knowledgable in the school and are perceived by all segments of the community as having a preventive effect on school vandalism. Frequently, staff from the YAC provide assistance to other security officers in identifying vandals.

About two years ago, the YAC model was endorsed by the Texas legislature through a bill that appropriated funds to establish such centers in ten other Texas communities. The key elements of the program's success include:

support for the program among cooperating agencies at all levels

school-based nature of the program

building on demonstrated success

credibility that flows from the use of "hard" money

The program has functioned effectively in a structure with a number of parallel authorities and reflects the fact that each agency has felt ownership at every level from the start of the program. Support by top-level officials has been very important in recruiting and retaining well-qualified staff, particularly among the police. The location of the YAC's services within school buildings and the central role of the teacher-in-charge have eased the acceptance of the program among school administrators. Furthermore, the program took place gradually, building on the positive experience of the initial schools. Finally, all those interviewed were convinced that the appropriation of local moneys to support the program has been critical to site acceptance across the city.

Alexandria, Virginia

Alexandria is largely residential suburban community across the river from Washington, D.C. Its school system has twenty-one public-school buildings and has an enrollment of 5,200 in grades 7 through 12 and 6,600 in the elementary grades and others. The system uses a building-security program, whose contact person is Dennis Leone, administrative assistant to the superintendent.

Creation of the Program

Alexandria, Virginia, has a school system well known to security directors. One of the first security-monitoring systems in the country was installed there in its twenty-one public-school buildings, to provide a quick response to the rapid rise in property damage. It was initially hoped that this approach would help to distinguish between burglaries and vandalism throughout the system. With the assistance of LEAA, Alexandria helped pioneer many innovative security systems currently used in numerous school systems nationwide.

Operation of the Program

The school-system center is located at T.C. Williams High School and is operated from a central switchboard in the school's main office. Security at T.C. Williams itself is handled through video monitoring, and the city's other twenty schools are on an audio system. The switchboard has a security officer watching and listening for any unusual incidents from 4 P.M. to 7 A.M. every school day and longer on weekends and holidays. The security system is six years old; currently more sophisticated units are available. However, for the size of the high school (approximately 1,700 students), the video-monitoring system was described by school personnel as being totally effective and adequate. The staff interviewed on our site visit believed that a more elaborate system was not needed to reduce school theft and vandalism in their schools. The directors in Alexandria have one strong recommendation to other schools shopping for security systems: ". . . test everything before you buy."

The high school, as part of its vandalism policy, also developed a restitution program, in which parents are liable for up to $200 for damage incurred at the school. Graffitti is quickly removed from bathrooms, and vandalism damage is repaired immediately to avoid the appearance of deterioration. There is, however, some concern in Alexandria that students are blamed for vandalism that may be caused by adults. In addition, school items are labeled, coded, painted, and bolted where possible.

If a school facility is unlawfully entered during nonschool hours, setting off the audio-monitoring system, the security aide at the switchboard in T.C. Williams calls the police. (Originally, Alexandria operated a roving patrol car, but this was not cost effective.) When the police enter the school, they are accompanied by dogs, which have on occasion been released.

The Police Department also discussed the importance of coordination with the schools. When the system was first installed, there were numerous false alarms, using up unnecessary police time. Within a year the number of false alarms was reduced to five per month. The policy and security staff worked out a common reporting system, a personal-emergency-contact system, and a routine-communication flow. Both the school and police were concerned that they lacked the strong support of the court. They believe this to be an essential ingredient of a successful program.

Impact of the Program

Several of the individuals we talked to felt that the security system gave them a greater sense of confidence and increased community involvement with the school. The entire security system installed for all the schools initially cost $64,203, of which $47,081 was funded through a grant from LEAA. Now approximately $8,000 to $10,000 is spent each year on maintenance and $27,000 for staff. CETA funds are used for additional security-support personnel.

Students did not seem to pay much attention to the cameras that observed them throughout the hallways at T.C. Williams; nor was the existence and presence of a security system an issue to the students with whom we talked. The principal informed the site-review team that the cameras provoked much resentment among students when they were initially installed even though they were not on during regular school hours.

In summary, the Alexandria system is practical and efficient and has stood the test of time. The security system works fine when the school is closed, but daytime harrassment and petty vandalism remain, causing frustration and irritation for the staff.

Escambia County, Florida

The Escambia County school district is a consolidated urban, suburban, and rural district near Pensacola, Florida, with sixty-five school sites and approximately 47,000 students. It uses a building-security program; the program's contact person is T.J. LeMaster, assistant superintendent.

Creation of the Program

Like other school districts, Escambia's revenues are stagnant if not shrinking. They view vandalism as robbery, and their security effort is a serious attempt to stop this raid on their treasury. In the early 1970s the district's vandalism problem was costing about $50,000 per year. All indications were that this cost would continue to increase. Additionally, the problems of student classroom misbehavior were on the rise. With this in mind, the district took several steps to effect a turn-around.

Specifically, the school district has developed two interesting approaches to reduce school vandalism, which they find very effective for their type of setting: trailer residences and security improvements and an interagency working agreement between court, school, and children's services.

Operation of the Program

Escambia County has placed mobile homes at thirty-one schools. Residents are provided a place to park their trailer homes and their utilities are paid ($100 or less per month) in exchange for twenty-four-hour coverage of the school grounds. A careful screening process has been established, but finding "acceptable" residents has been somewhat difficult. Applicants must not have other work that takes them away from the school grounds at night and must have a sincere desire to work with students. Finally, they must own their own trailer and be willing to move it onto campus.

Once on campus, these residents are encouraged to take an active part in school activities. In this way they get to know the students, and a mutual respect is formed. Often, individuals interviewed claimed that residents become active "parents" to the entire school. It is believed that the development of this sense of belonging is necessary to the program's success.

Trailer residents are required to check the school from the outside every evening. Residents do not have police powers nor do they carry weapons or wear uniforms. If vandalism does occur, they notify the police. Where the capability exists, an intercom is wired to the trailer and turned on as a continuous monitor at night. Aside from these few responsibilities, the residents go about their usual routine.

Other security options are in effect in Escambia. Fences have been placed around some schools to limit vehicular access; lighting has been installed to make monitoring by police, trailer residents, and citizens easier. Custodian work-hours have been shifted to later in the day; this provides an additional eight hours of coverage after school closes in the afternoon. Bulletins have been printed and distributed to the neighborhoods encouraging citizens to be "nosy" about people who are on campus after hours or students who are "hanging around," and off-duty police are regularly asked to beef up security, through a working agreement with the Pensacola Police Department. The Escambia County Sheriff's Auxiliary also provides extra security forces. Under the CETA Man-power Program, sixteen guards have been employed. The Sheriff's Department has deputized these guards so they have arrest powers. However, they do not carry weapons. Seven guards cover high schools exclusively. The remaining nine form a roving patrol and provide spot coverage twenty-four hours a day. Additionally, the Manpower Office has supplied fourteen senior citizens covering ten sites to act as security guards. They are deputized and have arrest powers.

In addition to these measures, a written manual has been prepared for the school department, the court, and the Division of Children and Youth Services to ensure a coordinated response to ungovernable, truant, or apprehended juvenile offenders. The school system provides a full-time liaison or visiting teacher. The job of the liaison is to assure that the school system is informed of the disposition of the referral and to present relevant information to the court.

Vital to the agreement is that a disposition will be reached in fifteen days. The first step is to decide if a judicial or nonjudicial disposition is necessary, based on the nature of the offense and the background of the child. Judicial solutions are sought only when the child has demonstrated that action outside the court is unlikely to halt the behavior. Again, the court, school, and youth-serving agency are partners in this decision.

The agreement has particularly well defined steps in relation to truant youth and juveniles who are "ungovernable" at school (students who "consistently reject authority in the school"). On the first adjudication, the student may be treated as a dependent child and placed under supervision of protective ser-vices. On the second and all subsequent adjudications, the juvenile may be treated as delinquent and placed on probation or committed to Youth Services.

Judicial solutions generally involve restitution when vandalism is the offense. Part of the judgment may require the child to perform certain tasks or a specific job to make restitution.

Impact of the Program

The Escambia County School District has tried several means to curb vandalism and student disruptions. The present superintendent and Board are 100 percent behind the programs now in use. They do seem to have very low costs and high effectiveness. However, to date Escambia has collected very little data bearing on security effectiveness.

Given the lack of available data and the somewhat unusual setting, the Escambia model cannot be broadly recommended at this time. Still, the novel approach taken by this school system bears close watching and suggests the potential for the creative use of resources.

Summary

Chapter 4 presented detailed case studies of six diverse school-vandalism programs. Each description discussed the origin of the program, how it actually operates, and its accomplishments and impact.

The programs began with an attempt to expand and coordinate youth-serving programs in Fresno County, California, to plan and deliver better preventive services to juveniles. The second case study described the Flint, Michigan, community schools, where extensive community and parent participation appears linked to low rates of vandalism.

A curricular and behavioral-change program in Madison, Wisconsin, was next. The program included decentralizing planning and encouraged local decision making, expanded interagency coordination around the issue of vandalism, and staff training and curriculum development. In Dallas, concern about growing school vandalism in one junior high school led to the creation of twenty-one youth action centers across the city. The centers encourage interagency coordination and improved service delivery to potential and actual vandals and to other troubled youth.

The fifth case study described Alexandria, Virginia's building-security program. A combined audiovisual-monitoring system allows one security officer to monitor twenty-one schools during all nonschool hours. The last case study discussed a trailer-resident program in Escambia County, Florida, that placed community residents full-time on the school grounds. It has been combined with improved interagency coordination to produce a comprehensive, broad-based vandalism program.

5

Designing a School-Vandalism- Prevention Program

In chapter 1, the likelihood that school administrators and board members would opt for the short-range political solutions appearing in the most readily available and tangible vandalism program was suggested. It was also suggested that such an approach can unleash unfortunate long-range side effects because of the complex and diverse causes that have been overlooked in the interests of haste. The first four chapters have outlined the current knowledge in the field, available options, and the experiences of a select number of other school districts. The purpose of this chapter is to propose a framework to help school administrators choose among the bewildering array of antivandalism options.

As much as administrators would like to have and all concerned would like to provide a quick answer to the vandalism problem in each district, no simple solutions are possible. A brief outline such as this cannot possibly take into account the enormous complexity of issues that confront school administrators every day. Nor can the idiosyncrasies of individual school systems be fully considered. Used as a guide, however, the framework proposed here can help school personnel select vandalism programs whose effects can be lasting, adaptable, and cost effective.

To this end, a developmental process is proposed that includes the following stages (figure 5-1): stage I: problem assessment; stage II: resource identification; stage III: program planning; and stage IV: program evaluation.

Problem Assessment

Vandalism crises are nearly always preceded by a sense of urgency in the schools and the community. There are reports in the media and letters and protests to the school superintendent and school board. Frequently a precipitating incident moves vandalism to the front burner: a major, deliberately set fire in a school facility; a newspaper exposé on the sad state of the school buildings; a public protest by staff; a budget report highlighting the cost of vandalism to the taxpayer.

Many school administrators have suggested that the risk, at this point, is to try to do too much too soon: buy the most readily available alarm system from the first salesman who appears, or announce that vandalism will be under control by year's end. Instead of rushing into a solution, administrators need to take the time and, sometimes, the flak that accompanies it and look carefully at the nature and severity of the problem.

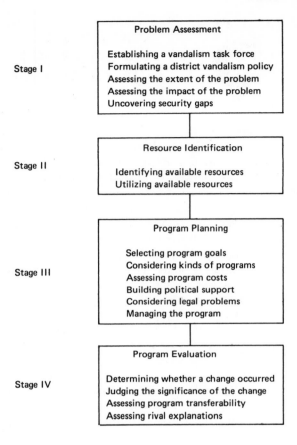

Figure 5-1. Vandalism-Prevention-Planning Process.

Here, as elsewhere, administrators will need all the help they can get. Certainly, a wide range of individuals and groups have a stake in reducing vandalism. These include teachers, staff, students, parents, community groups, business, political leaders, the police, and other youth-oriented agencies. It is important to involve all interested groups in finding a solution, and in making it work. Looking at the nature of the vandalism problem in your district makes a good starting point.

Establishing a Vandalism Task Force

One of the first things needed to address the vandalism problem is a task force or series of working groups, chaired by the superintendent or a board member. Establishing such a body in the first few days after the precipitating incident provides the tangible and visible assurance needed by the community. The task force should be named quickly and should include representatives from each of the groups previously mentioned. Specifically, one may want to consider the following groups for membership in the task force:

1. school-security personnel
2. teachers
3. school-board members
4. police
5. community youth agencies
6. business representatives
7. students
8. civil-rights groups
9. school-maintenance staff
10. counselors
11. administrative staff
12. parents
13. clergy
14. mayor's office
15. fire department

Choosing student members from both high-achieving and disenfranchised groups may help avoid the appearance of favoritism. Both groups will have to live with the results of the task force, and it is better to have their active involvement and support.

The issues of exactly whom to pick and of whether they are representative are always sensitive and crucial. Many would recommend that each group select its own representative, wherever possible, and that the list be supplemented as necessary.

How to recruit each of these groups for the task force is also an important issue. In districts that lack well-established community and other group relationships it is suggested that a sevenfold process be used to obtain each group's participation:

1. select the groups most needed for your task force and the size of the force
2. identify leaders or representatives for each group
3. establish the organizational protocol for each group
4. have the task-force leader or leader's designee phone the representatives, outline the issues and broad goals of the task force, who else is being asked to participate, and the need for their involvement
5. send a follow-up letter stating what was discussed on the phone and the date for the first meeting
6. have someone else selected for the task force telephone another potential member to offer moral support
7. telephone each member just prior to the meeting to confirm their attendance

The task force should meet as often as is necessary and should concentrate its work on policy formulation, problem assessment, resource examination, program planning, and program implementation and evaluation.

Formulating a District Vandalism Policy

Once the vandalism task force is in place, its first order of business should be to formulate a districtwide policy on property destruction. In addition to providing a guideline for the schools' response to vandalism, a formal policy will offer the community a clear signal that the task force is progressing and that its authority is serious. It may also help prevent some complaints against the district that might be lodged due to inconsistency in how the schools treat offenders. Lawsuits against school systems are becoming increasingly common; a well-publicized policy on school vandalism may prevent some litigation and may protect administrators and students when they do occur. It is suggested that once the policy has been drafted that it be turned over to the superintendent and/or school board for public comment and final adoption.

What goes into the policy statement is extremely important. It should, at the least, provide the district and the community a clear indication of the goals of your educational program, of those of your antivandalism efforts, and of how the two complement one another. Vestermark and Blauvelt (1978, p. 93) have recommended that the following issues be considered in the development of a districtwide security-policy statement:

1. the types of vandalism on which the district's program should target
2. long- and short-term objectives of the district's security program
3. general emphasis of the program; for example, police, guards, community groups, parents, hardware, or a mix of efforts
4. roles of the school board, superintendent, principals, community groups, security directors, police, teachers, and students
5. rights and responsibilities of each of these groups
6. special security problems to be considered in the program
7. school-district jurisdiction over property and land, boundaries, and the relationship with the metropolitan police
8. ultimate responsibility for security at each school
9. how violators or vandals will be treated for each kind of offense
10. resources that the district will invest in the effort

Other issues, of course, need to be considered and many are discussed throughout this chapter. A careful reading is suggested before a statement is approved by the school district.

Assessing the Extent of the Problem

The next issue that the task force must address is the nature and extent of the vandalism problem. Having information on what other districts are doing will be of little benefit if one has no firm grasp of your district's problems. A conclusion found in most national studies is that each school district and each school differ subtly but importantly in the exact nature of their damages. Designing an effective prevention program will rest heavily on the ability of the district to discern exactly where the problem lies.

To conduct an assessment the following general questions should be considered:

1. Is vandalism getting worse in the district?
2. Is vandalism following seasonal trends?
3. Does the nature of the problem vary from school to school?
4. Is the problem widespread or is it isolated in a few schools?
5. What kinds of acts are being committed?
6. What appear to be targets?
7. When does the problem seem most severe?
8. Who has been caught?

Scope of the Problem. The first aspect of the problem to be considered involves its scope. Just how widespread is the problem? Vandalism in one or a few isolated schools may have different significance than more dispersed destruction. Start the investigation by examining in detail the records at the district's security office or by asking individual principals to submit reports on damage in their schools. An accurate assessment will not be possible by simply listing the schools and the sum of each's damage. A number of pitfalls accompany vandalism data. The first among these involves the kinds of destruction. Not all destruction is of equal significance or impact, and therefore incidents cannot be added to form a total-vandalism index. It is best to keep separate figures on each type and avoid combining them. A sample form in appendix B has been designed to help develop a school-by-school profile of a district's vandalism problem. In large districts, select a sample of schools rather than doing an assessment of them all.

There are a number of statistical tools one can use to analyze these school-by-school figures, and it is best to consult your research director. If the district is without a research staff, add the school-by-school incidents and dollar losses for each offense. The totals for each offense should give a fair picture of which kinds of destruction are costing most on a districtwide basis. It may also be advisable to divide the schools by the grade levels they include. The second step involves choosing the top 10 or 15 percent of the schools in each offense category. Then, compare the results from one offense to another. Are the same schools listed consistently? Several schools listed repeatedly may indicate the need for having programs targeted for each school.

The incompatability of offense types is only one of the hazards in assessing property damage. Some of the offenses one encounters are so rare, for example, arson and bombings, that chance alone may account for apparent high incidence. Be careful with such figures because they can be misleading. If in doubt, check bombing and arson records for past years to see if any pattern arises.

A third hazard rests in the offense categories themselves. Be sure that the district's schools are reporting offenses in the same way. A clear set of instructions for each category can help.

In addition, simple counts of incidents may lead to inaccurate conclusions when the schools are of varying sizes and grade levels. Reporting incidents as a rate, that is, incidents per one hundred students, solves this problem to a large extent.

Although asking the security director or principals to report vandalism is one way to assess the district's problem, the task force may want to consider the use of a student or teacher survey. Again divide the results by grade level, offense, size, and individual school.

Examining which schools have what problems can be a money saver in the long run. There is no need to install a districtwide hardware system if only a few of your schools are repeatedly damaged. By this stage the task force should have a good grip on what acts are committed in which schools and can now proceed through the remainder of the assessment.

Trends of the Problem. The second aspect of the problem in need of examination involves trends. Is the destruction getting worse? When does the vandalism appear to be most severe? In the first part of the assessment, restrict questions to districtwide vandalism trends; then move to trends in individual schools. It is possible that there are a number of problems within the district, stemming from a variety of causes. Concentrate the examination on the following areas.

Year-to-Year Trends. From a policy standpoint the board will want to know whether or not vandalism is increasing. An answer to this question may be provided by comparing total dollar losses from year to year. Unfortunately, this approach has some problems. The first involves inflation. In general, dollars are a desirable base on which to figure vandalism losses, but the base changes from year to year because of changes in the cost of living. When comparing vandalism costs from one year to the next, inflation will dramatize current costs and deemphasize earlier ones (Rubel 1977b). Be sure to break the data down by elementary- and secondary-grade levels and by type of offense. It is not unusual to see theft rates rising while burglaries fall. When tracing vandalism trends from one year to the next, watch for changes in the ways schools report their destruction or policy changes on what is considered as vandalism. A third caution: be sure to correct the figures by changes in yearly enrollment. This is particularly important with enrollments declining as they are now. The easiest way to do this is to convert your raw data to incident-costs per student. A final aspect of year-to-year trends one may want to consider involves determining whether some of the vandalism in the district is "following" a particular individual or group. As bizarre as it sounds to academicians, most building-level educators know that some kids are a continuing terror throughout their careers in the district. Data over at least five years are needed to begin such an assessment.

Month-to-Month Trends. In addition to knowing whether or not the vandalism problem is growing worse, it is important that month-by-month trends be traced—especially if the district is located in the snowbelt. It may be advisable on the basis of the month-to-month analysis to augment security staff some months and decrease it during others. Like the annual trends, be sure to separate monthly trends by grade level and type of destruction. Also pay particular attention to months when the buildings are not in heavy use, that is, Christmas and summer holidays. It may be useful at this point to consult the district's statistician to correct annual vandalism rates by the monthly fluctuations in the amount and type of destruction.

Day-to-Day Trends. A third major type of data involves day-to-day trends. Are there particular days of the week that witness greater destruction? Is night destruction more severe than that during the day? Again, the significance of this information rests in deciding where to put the greatest programmatic emphasis. As with the other trends, break the data down by grade level, type of destruction, location, and month. You may also want some understanding of the relative risks of destruction run at varying times of the day (*Safe School Study* 1977) rather than knowing only the simple distribution of the vandalism. One way of doing this is by first calculating the percentage of destruction occurring during school hours and nonschool hours then dividing that percentage by the number of hours comprising that inschool or nonschool period. The ratio of the two periods is your risk per hour of experiencing destruction at various times. For example, suppose figures indicate that 5 percent of your destruction occurs during school hours and 95 percent occurs after school. If the total school week amounts to thirty-five hours, then 0.14 percent of your destruction occurs per hour during school and 2.7 percent during out-of-school periods—a 19 to 1 ratio or 19-times-greater-per-hour risk of destruction after school. You will probably want to calculate such a risk rate for each kind of destruction, and a rate for both afterhour weekday and weekend periods. In addition, breaking the data down by day of the week may be useful. From this kind of analysis it is possible to get a better handle on when and on what to focus the security budget and personnel. Improved efficiency in this area can save thousands of dollars.

Targets of the Destruction. Assumed throughout this handbook is that vandalism does not occur randomly. There is a reason for the destruction, no matter how bizarre or incomprehensible. One way of uncovering the nature of the vandalism problem involves analyzing not only the kinds of acts committed but also their targets. This might be particularly useful when one or a group of schools has experienced a sudden rash of incidents. The outbreaks may be accounted for by a simple change in school rules or the perceived arbitrary act of a single teacher. Broken windows or "trenched" school yards may have nothing particularly significant in them—other than a generalized disregard for the school—but other acts like repeated trashing of the gym teacher's equipment may.

Miscellaneous. In addition to those aspects of the problem just discussed, there are others worth investigating. Be sure to interview those individuals who have been caught destroying property to see if there are insights to be gained about their behavior. Secondly, investigate the nature of the destruction to see if there are patterns in certain sections of the district or other things about the school and its surrounding neighborhood that might contribute to the vandalism. The *Safe School Study* (1977) uncovered a slight relationship between some acts and how close students lived to school. (More will be presented on other physical aspects of the school building later.) A third possible avenue for investigation seems obvious—ask the students. A simple anonymous survey of their own victimization or participation may do. Finally, if the district has a fairly sophisticated research staff, ask them to research various aspects of school climate and the relation to property destruction.

By now the task force should be getting a fair picture of what the district is up against. In sum, get as much information as is possible by school, type of offense, grade level, month, time of day, and targets. Your thoroughness in this tedious task will be worthwhile in the long run.

Assessing the Impact of the Problems

Once the dimensions of the problem are more clearly understood, the task force should go on to look at the impact of the vandalism. Many acts of vandalism may be much less harmful than a few: twenty broken bathroom partitions are less destructive than one large fire. Similarly, incidents spread across the system may have less damaging educational impact than a few acts concentrated in two or three schools.

Unfortunately, there is no simple statistical method to be recommended that will give a complete assessment. It must be, for the most part, judgmental. The task force may want to consider the following kinds of effects vandalism may be having:

1. Financial cost is the estimated dollar losses of vandalism in individual schools (see earlier section). Be careful of the hazards previously mentioned in analyzing cost data.

2. Education cost is the impact of vandalism on the process of teaching and learning in each school and on the system as a whole. The task force will need to talk to a variety of staff, students, parents, and community leaders to arrive at an estimate of severity. This cost is particularly judgmental, for there is no way to quantify the educational impact that mutilated classroom animals have, for example, on third graders.

3. Political cost is the loss of control over daily events by school administrators because of the destruction. The political effect of vandalism is often ignored in developing program options. Over an extended period, this problem can be extremely serious when the perceived leadership ability of the administration wanes. Once again, this is a judgment call, but it is worth the consideration of the task force.

4. Law-enforcement cost is the loss of positive relationships between the schools and the various law-enforcement agencies as a result of extensive vandalism. These agencies include the police, probation office, courts, and youth-service bureaus that may have responsibility for identified vandals.

With each of these costs, the task force should consider both the immediate and long-range impact of the destruction. A major building fire, for instance, may have great immediate effect on the entire system; with improved fire-detection devices, however, the long-term impact of building fires may be minimal. Conversely, a rash of wastebasket fires in several schools during class time may have little short-term impact; over a long period, however, they may seriously harm the teaching staff's ability and willingness to teach.

There is a limit on the ability of this or any work to tell you exactly how to assess the impact of your specific vandalism problem. A thorough and reasoned discussion of the various kinds of costs the damage has, however, should provide a clearer idea of the measures needed to alleviate the problem.

Uncovering Security Gaps

Whether the district has a full-fledged security program or is just developing one, the task force will probably want to make sure that all the inexpensive safety measures have been taken care of in the schools. For the most part these measures involve the kinds of basic target-hardening efforts discussed in chapter 3.

There are any number of ways such an assessment might be done, but one particularly impressive aid was developed by the Educational Facilities Laboratory for the American Association of School Administrators (AASA).

In appendix C is included a revised checklist from the AASA material on assessing school buildings for their overall vulnerability to damage. The check list allows one to determine in detail the likelihood of repeated property losses in play areas, informal-gathering spots, outdoor areas, shrubbery, lavatories, cafeterias, shops, doors, windows, fixtures, gyms, ceilings, floors, rooftops, and walls. This form was designed for use at the building level and might be advocated for structures suffering chronic untargeted damage. Many of the items are simply preventive in nature and generally inexpensive.

Identifying gaps in the security system requires a similar kind of assessment. Chances are that your security program was designed some years ago and may be in need of a checkup. If this is the case, supplement the assessment just described with one targeted on your vandalism program. Consider a full-fledged evaluation to see if the program is working the way it was intended. More on program evaluation will be included in the last section of this chapter. In the meantime, a quick assessment may be all that is needed. Appendix B contains another checklist of things to consider about your program. The list is fairly general but covers many of the things considered important if the simplest of programs can be expected to work. The task force will need to have the data from the problem assessment; it is possible that the district's program is no longer in sync with the current vandalism problem.

At this point, the task force should have a reasonably clear idea of where the vandalism problem lies, how extensive the effect of the damage is, and how well the security system is targeted. The critical thing to remember at this point is that an effective program to reduce vandalism will be impossible to design without solid information. Lacking that information, those responsible for the safety and security of the children and staff must make program decisions on a very precarious basis.

The task force is now ready to start planning the program.

Resource Identification

The second phase of the information-collection process involves identifying resources. Too often, school systems define their resources only in terms of budgeted dollars and staff. It is essential that the task force range as widely as possible in considering what is available to fight vandalism. Not only should new ways of obtaining funds be considered (for example, the use of CETA funds to pay for security guards) but also new school practices needing little to no capital outlay should be examined.

One of the best ways to start thinking creatively about resources is to consider the vandalism problem as broadly as possible. What other problems are similar or related to vandalism? The problem assessment may have uncovered issues related to drugs and alcohol, youth unemployment, truancy, staff morale, student rights, lack of instructional facilities, and others. Addressing these and other problems may bring to mind federal, state, and community resources. To help in this area, see appendix A of this book.

In addition, think as comprehensively as possible about the various sources of help. The federal government, for instance, has authorized vandalism-related financial assistance through the Safe Schools Amendment to the Elementary and Secondary Education Act (ESEA) (Title IX, Part D) and technical assistance through the LEAA-sponsored School Resource Network. Other federal assistance is available, however, through programs not directly related to vandalism. The Youth Employment and Training Program (CETA, Title IV), the Public Service Employment Program (CETA, Title II), the Alternative Schools Project (LEAA), the Public Works Program, and the Community Development and Housing Program are examples of sources of funds not often tapped by schools. Other federal resources include Energy grants under the Energy Conservation Act (Title III), the National Endowment for the Arts and the National Endowment for the Humanities, and Building Conservation programs sponsored by the Department of Interior. There are also more traditional grant sources like Title IV of ESEA, and the Special Project monies under Emergency School Aid that might be used in part to address the property damage. A look through the *Domestic Assistance Catalogue* might help uncover other sources. State sources of funding are often available through similar programs.

At the local level, there is not only the mayor's office but usually a host of community-based organizations that may be able to provide program funds or expertise. Do not overlook the business community and local foundations for support. School systems in Chicago, Milwaukee, and Dade County are good examples of districts that tapped their local community for funding. Most larger cities have small foundations designed specifically to provide seed money for local projects. *The Annual Register of Grant Support*, a publication available at the local public library, may help in locating some of these foundations and what they are interested in funding.

Financial help is the most commonly thought of aid in developing programs but there are organizational and human resources as well. The local youth-service bureau, television station, child-care agency, family-counseling service, athletic teams, fraternal order of police, bar association, and others may have services to draw on at extremely low cost. In addition, they may be able to refer one to other organizations—both traditional and alternative.

Also include in your planning the local college as a source of technical skills. Lastly, be sure to consider the human resources and talents of the students, staff, and parents: the local PTA provides direct access to talented people in the community who have their children in the public schools.

A final way to consider resources is by trying to match up community needs. Is there some problem the school district has that might be solved by solving someone else's problem? Programs locating mobile homes on school grounds demonstrate a problem (vandalism) being addressed by providing low-cost housing (someone else's problem). Dade County provides another example. That school system has employed unemployed parents—using CETA funds—to act as security personnel and counselors in particularly troubled schools. It is an approach that borrows on the ancient system of bartering, and the task force may be able to come up with any number of good ideas. The possibilities are endless.

If the task force has followed the steps described, it will now have identified the nature of the vandalism problem, assessed its complexity, and examined resources to respond to the situation. It is now ready to put all this information to use.

Program Planning

The third stage of program development is likely to be the hardest, for it involves synthesizing all the information collected so far. Besides knowing the nature, impact, and whereabouts of the vandalism problem, the task force will need to consider factors like the community distaste for one particular kind of program versus another, political support for various program strategies, immediate and long-range cost and legal problems. In addition, there are management problems to consider. To start this process, make sure that the task force has all the objective data gathered to date and the general advantages and disadvantages of the many program types described in chapter 3. Then, move through the following sections to help shape the formation of the prospective program.

Selecting Program Goals

Before designing the specifics of the program, the task force will need to decide on program goals. Certainly, the overall goal will be to reduce vandalism; but as we have seen, the problem is likely to look different depending on the school being considered. As with most other education programs, the goals for the antivandalism effort should be as measurable as possible. This means stating the goals for the program in terms of either dollars or incidents. Beware of the hazards with these measures that were discussed earlier. State the objectives for both the long term, say a three-year period, and short term (the end of the next school year). In addition, break the objectives down into expectations for reducing each kind of property destruction identified in the problem assessment. The task force should set specific objectives in terms of dollars lost or incidents for the target schools and an overall districtwide set of goals. Consider also setting goals and objectives around issues indirectly related to vandalism, for example, absenteeism, assaults, extracurricular participation, and parental involvement. Problems of evaluation will be discussed later in this chapter, but it is not unreasonable to think that other related issues will be affected by whatever antivandalism program is set into motion. To help in the goal-setting process, a series of resources are included in appendix A.

After program goals are selected, review them to see whether or not they are congruent with the general educational goals of the district. It is not uncommon for districts to develop programs that actually work against the long-range academic and other social goals of the school system and the community.

Considering Kinds of Programs

Outlined in chapter 3 are many programs that school districts throughout the country are testing. The list is by no means exhaustive, and each district ought to think through program options that fit their district best. To start, though, the task force might look back through the lists of advantages and disadvantages for each program type included in chapter 3. Again, it is likely that the task force will want to consider different program strategies in various parts of the district, depending on what the needs assessment uncovered. Now is the time to start consolidating the information collected on the nature of the problem, on available resources, and on program goals. Some options may be eliminated immediately should the nature of the problem warrant it. For instance, if the assessment has uncovered a serious problem with arson, it may be possible to eliminate some target-hardening strategies. At this point, it is important to keep the broadest perspective possible on the kinds of programs under consideration.

Assessing Program Costs

If the list of program options can be narrowed to five or so, the next central question will involve cost. Also in need of consideration will be the relative cost efficiency of the program after it has been in operation a year.

The issue of cost in choosing among programs is especially important because many security measures are so expensive that a mistake can cause a tremendous drain on a district's resources. Unfortunately, cost-benefit technology has not yet been successfully applied to the vandalism field. Directly comparing the costs or the degree of effectiveness of the various kinds of programs yields little. Not all are designed for the same purpose. Building-security programs focus primarily on night and weekend or holiday damage. Target-hardening and architectural programs are addressed in large measure to accidental or nonmalicious damage. Community relations emphasize neighborhood involvement in school activities; offender-accountability programs target their efforts at changing student behavior; and institutional and curriculum projects focus on long-range organizational and educational goals.

Because each kind of program is normally designed to address a slightly different purpose, the task force will probably not be looking to decide whether to choose between hardware systems and human relations. More likely the question will be, "What is the most cost-effective community project?" or "Which alarm system is most cost-efficient?" To help answer these questions, take into account a number of costs.

Acquisition Costs. These are the one-time costs incurred while setting up the program (Haggart 1971). They involve the expenses associated with acquiring the capability to run the program and include such things as:

Costs of Designing the Program. In this case, the costs are the salaries for those planning the program, transportation, and outside consultants. These costs tend to run higher with security programs because of their technical nature and your need to rely on outside help. Consultant costs can also run high for human-relations programs. To cut costs in this category, the district may be able to rely on its own inhouse expertise, a local university, or the business community.

Costs for Developing Materials. These costs include the design and printing of program brochures, curriculum materials, newsletters, training aids, and the like. These costs, of course, will run higher in programs involving curriculum changes or training packages for security personnel in the intricacies of a new alarm system. They will be considerably less in programs like target hardening, behavioral change, or architectural renewal, where there is less need for written materials. If you are considering a community-based effort, you may want to develop a neighborhood newsletter or flyer to keep people appraised of the program's progress. These should also be taken into account in tallying potential program costs.

Costs Associated with Evaluating the Program. These costs include staff salaries, meeting time, and outside evaluators. It cannot be stressed too much the importance of including an evaluation component in the program plan. You may be able to rely on the research and development staff of the district or recruit a willing graduate student in evaluation methodology from the local university. Naturally, costs increase if you seek the help of a consulting group. There is however, no particular reason why the costs of planning an evaluation should depend on the kind of program you are considering, unless you are undertaking a number of programmatic options. In that case, planning will be more difficult, and more costly.

Costs of Initial Service Delivery. These costs will usually be minimal to nothing, unless there is a startup fee attached to the alarm system being purchased.

Equipment Costs. These costs include typewriters, recorders, audiovisual machines, pocket alarms, television monitors, any security hardware, athletic equipment, buses, locks, watchdogs, or whatever. These costs will run considerably higher with security programs. In fact, the major difference in costs between security programs and all others rests in this category.

Costs of Materials and Supplies. Books, stamps, paper, literature reviews, games, films, accounting sheets, and the like are included here. These costs will include not only programmatic materials but the administrative supplies needed for managing the program. Programs involving community relations, human relations, and curriculum innovation will have higher costs in this category.

Costs of Preservice Training. These costs cover training for teachers, security guards, police, administrators, and custodians. This training can involve the use of new curricula materials, new security measures and policies, and vandalism-prevention techniques. Most expensive in this category are programs that stress security, curriculum, or human relations.

Cost of Facilities. Costs associated with renting, leasing, remodeling space, purchase of new space, and the like are included here. These costs tend to run high in programs where mobile homes are moved onto the campus as part of the security effort. Still, the costs run only a few thousand dollars at most. Be sure to include the costs of space for administrative staff.

Costs of Installation. These include the costs of installing hardware systems, lexan windows, locks, target-hardening measures, lighting systems, and the like. Not only will these costs be high for security and target-hardening programs but also for architectural-change efforts. Costs of installing displays or signs should also be considered.

It is customary that the acquisition costs listed be calculated on a per-program basis that is, one program versus another. Along with considering initial costs, the task force will want to consider costs that accompany the maintenance of the program:

Operational Costs. These are costs associated with running the program, including the costs of modifying program components and maintaining program capabilities. They include:

Program Activity Costs. These costs cover such things as program direction, evaluation, media services, management support, transportation, and other contracted services like insurance.

Salaries. Salaries to security forces, overtime for teachers involved in special antivandalism activities, fringe benefits, and the salaries of other specialists, administrators, and paraprofessionals are counted. Those costs, of course, will be higher in labor-intensive programs like those using security guards or contract security forces.

Inservice Training. These costs include training time, salaries for special trainers, facilities and materials needed to conduct training sessions, along with the salaries of the participants. The shorter the life of the various components of the proposed program, the more these costs will mount up. In addition, consider employee turnover and its effect on inservice training. A contract security force may have more turnover, for instance, and therefore require more frequent training sessions.

Materials and Supplies. The costs of updating, modifying, repairing, or restocking materials, pamphlets, manuals, paper, are included here. Some material such as films, human-relations curricula, and games can become outmoded and unpopular within two to three years. Pamphlets on the purposes of the program and the need for community support have a considerably longer life and will add relatively fewer costs.

Equipment. These costs include repairing, replacing, or maintaining program equipment such as burglar-alarm systems, television monitors, film projectors, and the like. These costs can be substantial in hardware-oriented programs.

Facilities. The costs of rent, mortgage, leasing overhead, utilities, and the like are covered. Again, these costs can be higher in programs like those that use mobile homes on campus. Programs that emphasize the illumination of the school grounds will need to be examined closely because of utility costs, as will programs that keep school buildings open for community use.

Miscellaneous Costs. These costs include daily transportation, media services, petty cash, false alarms, and the like.

Traditionally, most of these operational costs are figured on a per-student, per-staff-member, or per-unit basis. Keep in mind a number of other factors when considering operating-program costs, including such things as maintenance agreements from the company installing a hardware system; replacement and repair difficulties in case the system should break down; length of time needed before replacement parts can be obtained; insurance costs and the nature of the coverage provided by the policy; warranties on equipment; amortization and depreciation rates; long-term costs; and the life cycle of equipment, booklets, materials, training aids, and films.

In addition, the expected gains from the proposed program should be considered alongside the initial and operating costs.

Financial Gains. These are reimbursements or savings expected as a result of implementing the proposed program:

1. Insurance reimbursements for damaged property can be gained. Unfortunately, many school systems, especially the larger urban districts, are their own insurors and can expect no other forms of reimbursement.

2. Restitution payments from students, parents, or staff for damaged property can be counted.

3. There should be savings associated with the effectiveness of the program, including declines in money spent for repairing or replacing damaged school property, and in time and money spent running a vandalism program.

The task force will need to compare program options in somewhat greater detail, but these general categories should provide a start. To figure the total cost of a given program over the course of a calendar year, fiscal year, or school year, simply subtract annual savings due to the program from its annual operating costs. The relative cost efficiency of one program versus another involves nothing more than dividing profits (the difference between annual gains and costs) by the annual operating costs of the programs.

Building Political Support

At this point, the task force should have a fair picture of the kinds of programs that would be most appropriate for the district—given its dollars, other resources, and problems. It is important at this stage to begin exploring the degree of political support from various community constituents for each of the program options. Lack of teacher support for a human-relations curriculum, for instance, is likely to ensure program failure.

Considering Legal Problems

There have not been, to date, many court cases on the problems of school vandalism and the programs aimed at reducing it. It is conceivable, though, that this hiatus will not continue for long. Already the courts have become heavily involved in student-rights cases and will likely be deciding on issues that span the entire range of educational problems. Both students and parents are significantly more aware of their rights under the law than at any other time in the history of schooling. The district's attorney should be brought in at this stage to assess possible legal problems with the programs being considered.

One of the few areas in which legal cases have appeared involves that of discipline. The 1975 Supreme Court decision of Goss v. Lopez (419 U.S. 565) assured students the right to due process in any disciplinary procedure. The intent behind the decision was to uphold individual student rights to a free education. So far, that intent has been defined rather narrowly, but a broader interpretation of the law may someday be tested. In addition, the High Court ruled in 1977 in the case of Ingraham v. Wright (438 U.S. 651) that corporal punishment for a school infraction did not violate either the eighth or the fourteenth amendments. The decision was based on the legal concept of "cruel and unusual punishment," which has not as far as we can tell been applied to practices like restitution for damaged school property. Third, a number of cases have tested the right of the school to "search and seizure" of student property. Although often used for alleged drug offenses, some legal standards might be applied to student bombs or fire-setting paraphenelia. Finally, students in California recently won a decision (*White* v. *Davis*) before the state's supreme court prohibiting the use of undercover agents to spy on student activities.

Suspensions, corporal punishment, search and seizure, and undercover agents involve less programmatic options than they do district or building-level-policy options. Almost no cases exist where someone has tested such possibilities as television monitors and student privacy, closed school buildings and community access to public property, architectural changes to reduce destruction and access for the handicapped, police in the schools and freedom of movement. Settled out of court was one case involving a guard dog that had attacked an innocent student in the hallway of a school. Such problems are rare, but the district's legal staff should be consulted to assess the potential for future legal headaches or consult with the National Organization on Legal Problems in Education (NOLPE) in Washington, D.C., or the Center for Law and Education in Cambridge, Massachusetts. The Resource Guide contains additional resources.

Managing the Program

Before the Task Force decides on which program(s) to implement, consideration should be given to the management aspects of the new effort. How will the program fit into the organizational structure of the school? Who will take responsibility for the program's success or failure? Who will run the program on a day-to-day basis? What will be the roles of the school staff? It should be pointed out here that school security, in whatever form the school board chooses to implement it, remains a support function under the general goal of educational achievement. Given this assumption, those charged with maintaining the overall educational standards of the district should most appropriately shoulder the responsibility for school security.

In an excellent new work, *Controlling Crime in the School*, the authors emphasize that personnel hired specifically for security duties should be placed in support of educators who set the general tone and style for a school system. It is almost always useful to have a separately operated security office that can respond quickly to problems rather than an ad hoc security group, but the office should be answerable to the district's educators. The authors further stress the need to clarify the security roles for all school staff, including principals, teachers, counselors, and custodians. Principals should be encouraged to communicate regularly with building-level staff on security problems, discuss recommendations with staff on how security violations are handled, and to press charges against vandals when they are identified. Teachers and counselors should be encouraged to inform the principal of security violations, be available for testimony, and make recommendations to improve overall safety of the buildings.

As part of the management plan, the task force will also need to consider developing—if the district does not already have one—a regularly maintained data-collection mechanism to help monitor the program and the vandalism problem. Also, be sure that the security office has a well-defined series of objectives, organizational responsibilities, and job descriptions.

Program Evaluation

The survey of school districts conducted as part of this work found that most had never formally evaluated their antivandalism efforts. However, a well-done evaluation is essential if the selection of program strategies is to be as reasoned as it should be. The intricacies of program evaluations cannot possibly be detailed in this short space, but the kinds of questions a critical evaluator will ask of the program to determine whether or not it has been successful can be summarized. Questions are drawn from an excellent new handbook published by NIE's Joint Dissemination Review Panel (JDRP), called *Ideabook*. (See Resource Guide, Program Evaluation.)

Determining Whether a Change Occurred

The first step in judging whether your program has been a success involves answering the query, "Did anything happen?" Using the program measures or indicators developed earlier, the evaluation will need to establish whether or not there was a change in the occurrence or cost of vandalism over the course of the program. The second part of the answer involves determining how that change was related to the program's objectives. This, of course, does not preclude unexpected side effects.

One of the first tasks in the evaluation is to link in logical fashion the vandalism program to the changes in destruction that occurred. The vagaries of nature result in changes in the state of things. The evaluation needs to discriminate between changes that occurred as a consequence of the program and those that did not. And one needs to link those changes to salient features of the program, not only side effects. This is done by simply connecting logically the expected and actual results.

To demonstrate that a change occurred it is insufficient to show that conditions after the program are different from those before the program. Instead, it must be shown that conditions could not have been achieved in the absence of the program. A simple before-after comparison will not convince many. The traditional way to demonstrate genuine change is through the use of a classical experimental design or some reasonable quasi-experimental substitute.

The chief problems are likely to be the absence of stable vandalism measures and of an equivalent control group. Again, one is cautioned about the hazards in the use of vandalism data. As for the second problem, the research office should be consulted about how to form similar but unequivalent control groups.

Judging the Significance of the Change

The significance of the change witnessed by the district can be judged in two ways: statistically and subjectively. The first is, of course, more technical and is beyond the scope of this report to tackle but the second is a matter of judgment. Two things need to be considered in this process. One involves the size of the effect and the second involves the importance of the area in which the change occurred, both at reasonable cost. A massively structured $2 million program of alarm systems, security officials, and target hardening can hardly be said to be significant, for instance, if it reduces destruction by only $3,500 per year. Assuming that the district's financial resources are limited, one is always better off selecting a low-cost program rather than a high-cost one, when the results are comparable. There are instances, of course, when cost cannot be the sole criterion. In cases of low-financial/high-social-cost vandalism like racial graffiti, it may be important to have invested additional funds to avoid the negative educational effects.

To further complicate matters, the task force will need to keep in mind that the program—if uniformly applied—will have different levels of effect depending on the type of child in the school, the surrounding neighborhood, degree of community support, and history of vandalism. Things only get worse when it has been decided to pursue a number of strategies aimed at reducing various kinds of vandalism, all with differing causes. Again, it will be a judgment call on the part of the task force to determine just how significant changes are expected to be.

Assessing Program Transferability

The term transferability asks whether the program can be duplicated in other schools at another time. If the district will consider expanding its program over the coming years, the task force will want to ask about the uniqueness of the program setting now or in the future. Is the program being planned likely to be successful due to its newness and the enthusiasm of newly hired staff? What happens in the doldrums of the program's second year? One should be prepared to demonstrate that the expected success of the program can be replicated next year, with new people in new schools. The best way to do this is to make sure that an evaluation is built into the program plan.

Another aspect of the transferability issue involves individual program components. The evaluators will want to build in a way of telling whether the important components of the program were implemented in the way the task force envisioned.

Assessing Rival Explanations

The purpose of any evaluation is to attempt to come up with the most plausible explanation for what happened. Explaining a changed world as a result of the program is a matter usually of good design work. It is very important that, during this part of the program planning, the task force structures the program in such a way that it can be evaluated without the clutter of rival explanations. A well-designed evaluation will pay for itself many times over in the amount of knowledge it yields and in the district's heightened ability to correct program flaws down the road.

You should be in a good position now to finalize a strategy that will have the greatest chance of success.

Summary

This chapter proposed a framework to help school administrators develop and select an effective, cost-efficient vandalism-control program. Four stages of program development are discussed: problem assessment, resource examination, program planning, and program evaluation.

First, the superintendent or school board was advised to establish a vandalism task force, broadly representative of school personnel, security specialists, parents, students, and the community. The task force assists the administration in establishing a vandalism policy for the district, and in assessing the extent, scope, characteristics, and impact of the problem.

Next, all available and potential financial, staff, parent, student, and community resources should be identified. Carefully defined and targeted program goals are developed, and the range of program options outlined in chapter 3 is weighed against program needs. Potential costs and benefits of each type of program are assessed in terms of the needs and goals of the school and district. A program or programs is selected, and a management plan and team defined, with clearcut responsibilities and lines of communication.

Finally, the superintendent and board need to formulate an evaluation plan for the program, which will clearly identify changes in vandalism rates and costs that result directly and indirectly from the antivandalism program.

6 Summary and Conclusions

Throughout this book we have tried to present a clear picture of school vandalism: theories, research, program analyses, promising approaches, and local-project development. The authors examined hundreds of articles on the subject, interviewed dozens of officials, and conducted a mail survey of one thousand local school systems. Much of the literature is reflected in the bibliography, the interviews in the case studies, and the research reviews included as earlier chapters of this work.

Chapter 1 provided an historical overview and discussed the major theoretical perspectives used to explain vandalism. We examined common approaches to defining vandalism, that is, according to its nature, intent, and costs, concluding the imprecision has contributed immensely to the confusion in the field. We also say from our own survey results that the ambiguity in the literature simply mirrored the inconsistencies in local reporting.

Chapter 2 took a detailed look at major research studies, starting with the controversial, localized studies of the 1960s and ending with the empirically based national *Safe School Study* of 1977.

The research revealed that, nationally, vandalism has leveled off at relatively high levels over the last seven to eight years; that specific targets are usually hit in a building (often repeatedly) by students of normal capacities and faculties who are usually enrolled in the damaged schools; that the season and time of day have a significant bearing on what is hit when; and that schools with particular styles of discipline (or lack thereof) are most frequently damaged.

Chapter 3 summarized program strategies that are most often used to address property destruction. In general, the program types could be categorized as environmental, which attempted to alter or protect the physical structure of the school; behavioral, aimed at modifying or changing student behavior; and systemic, targeted at the institutional policies of the school. Advantages and disadvantages of each program type were presented, and the range of options usually considered by schools in designing these programs were described.

Chapter 4 examined six diverse school systems and how they were working to rid themselves of excess property destruction. Community, institutional, security, curricular, behavioral, and human-relations strategies in these six districts were described. No specific conclusions were reached, but it was clear after visiting each site that what made them innovative and successful was that each project was thoroughly planned and implemented by a wide range of local people after taking into consideration many alternative strategies.

Chapter 5 was written to bring most of what is known about school vandalism together in practical proposals for dealing with property destruction. A process was proposed that included careful assessment, resource examination, program planning, and evaluation. It was emphasized that to be successful a program would need to be as complex as the problem itself.

A number of conclusions stand out to us at this point. The first involves who designs the programs. Young people are the most frequent vandals. Our work indicates, however, that more often than not it is administrators and school security personnel who, alone, design the antivandalism program. Only 23 percent of the districts responding to our survey said they directly involved students in planning or operating their vandalism effort, and only 15 percent indicated that they consulted with community groups in planning or making operating decisions. Few of the programs we described in this book were designed with any broad-based participation, but all groups in and outside the school community are touched one way or another by the results of the program. Although the administrators pay the bills for the destruction, it is the students and teachers who are affected most severely, both academically and psychologically. In addition, vandalism and other serious crimes paint a terribly grim picture of the competence of the schools. The exodus from the public schools, especially in urban areas, shows a basic lack of confidence in the quality of education and in the safety of their children. Property damage in the schools spells both poor quality and danger to parents and community leaders. This is one of the strongest reasons for involving these groups, along with students, in planning a safer and more responsive school system. The long-term success of the program and the schools will likely depend on it.

Furthermore, nearly all the school systems we examined had program strategies that fell within the same family. That is, building-security programs were apt to be found alongside target-hardening ones, target hardening with architectural design, offender-accountability programs with behavioral-change efforts, and human-relations with community-relations strategies. We think that this narrow response range limits the school's ability to respond effectively to a complex, multifaceted problem. First, schools should involve a broader group of people in program planning. Second, school systems should examine a wider range of program strategies. Third, schools should spend more time assessing the precise nature of the destruction. It is difficult to believe that vandalism in any school district is so homogeneous in its composition.

A third point involves the programs themselves. There is little evidence to indicate which of the programs described in this book are most effective in reducing particular kinds of property destruction. Most experts seem to agree that if night destruction and break ins have become a real problem, then building-security programs are probably the best bet. On the other hand, day destruction might just as effectively be met with programs using security, community, or student patrols. In either case, there is good reason to believe that target hardening will help reduce annoying, small-scale, needless destruction like glass breakage and graffiti. Problems related to the disruption of school routine may be harder to solve: although they require target hardening of fire alarms, for instance, they also necessitate removing the source of the disruption from the temptation of the students. Disruptions, however, usually require exceedingly simple behaviors to produce inordinately large results. The simple behaviors may be controlled by hardening such things as fire alarms, but the dramatic results of setting off a fire alarm might also be dissipated by fail-safe means to assure that no fire has actually been set, thus heading off any reflex evacuation of the buildings.

It is also difficult to know for sure which kind of program within any given family is best at reducing vandalism. No data exist, for instance, that say that community patrols are more effective than student patrols or that local alarms are more effective than detection ones. At this point, one is better guided by the intangible advantages and disadvantages we highlighted in chapter 3 and the general cost considerations discussed in chapter 5.

It is important to comment on differences in program strategies between urban and nonurban districts. On the whole, urban districts rely more heavily on security systems than other districts. Data from the *Safe School Study* and other research seem to indicate that vandalism is as severe in the suburban areas as it is in the cities, yet the suburban schools have not turned as often to building-security measures. There are probably two reasons for this. The first is that the urban districts have seen a greater expansion in the school-security profession, along with other professions, than smaller school systems. Secondly, the urban districts are more likely to face crimes against persons, which require many of the same security devices as property-related offenses. The lesson here is not so much that urban districts require or have reason to have more security but that their range of program selection has been surprisingly narrow.

Programs are often developed with short-term goals in mind, such as fewer broken windows and false alarms or decreased maintenance costs. This is both natural and sensible, but long-term educational goals also need to be considered. A vandalism program that has been designed to address that immediate problem but works against the school's educational goals has little chance of ultimate success. Some argue that any security effort works to the benefit of children and youth by increasing their safety and therefore improving their education. But it is also true that some security measures present such a prisonlike atmosphere that they work to the detriment of the schools' long-term academic goals. Vestermark and Blauvelt (1978) point out that to be effective over the long term a security office and its staff should remain a support function within the school structure. The security program should be built and managed to complement the basic educational role of the schools.

Next, the literature and the data that have been gathered so far indicate that it is inaccurate to think of vandalism and its vicitimized schools in homogeneous terms. Vandalism has served as a convenient rubric for classifying a host of often unrelated offenses. As we saw in chapter 1, some local school districts classify offenses as widely diverse as littering and bombings under the same category. But if research has indicated anything, it has shown that both the crime and the victim vary tremendously. The result of the traditional conceptualizations of vandalism has been deceiving incident rates and undeviating program strategies.

There is little uniformity or consistency in the way school districts define or report vandalism, in addition to inappropriate categorizing of vandalism incidents. The statistical impact of the inconsistencies is rather disconcerting. For the last several years, theories of causation, arguments over the extent of the problem, and vandalism-reduction programs have been built on the shakiest of statistical foundations. The likelihood that administrators would agree on standard terms is, of course, small. The crux of the problem involves, instead, common methods for tallying incidents and costs. Local school districts should probably continue defining vandalism in whatever way suits their needs. What might be useful, though, are consistent categories of vandalism acts and costs built into each reporting system. This would allow districts flexibility in categories and would give program design and evaluation information that is relatively uniform. There have been a number of attempts through the years to build common systems, with limited success. The difficulty of the task should not deter future efforts, however. As it stands, much of the data on vandalism and its costs are simply uninterpretable.

Another difficulty behind the accurate estimation on vandalism rates involves motive. Only within the last few years has much attention been given to motivational factors influencing crime reporting in the schools and the kinds of crimes committed. The fear of retribution from parents or central office staff, anxiety over lawsuits, the desire to protect one's reputation, and other factors all work to push vandalism rates artificially low. On the other hand, school-system program-funding mechanisms are sometimes tied to crime rates, encouraging higher reporting. In addition, only recent attention has been given to motivation underlying the crimes themselves. We have to date a number of conceptual approaches to vandalism that take into account the intent and effect of the behavior, but the theories lack verification. They do represent a start, however, and deserve the slow and steady process of winnowing needed to build a comprehensive theory of school-property destruction. Motivational factors, in combination with unstandardized definitions and various statistical problems, make the true nature of the problem hard to gauge.

A final point we would like to make involves causation. The pattern of property destruction in schools is hardly random. There is a dynamic—not yet fully understood—underlying the damage that is partly explained by knowing the season, time of day, and the area of the school. It cannot be reasonably concluded from the research that vandalism happens on a chance basis. There are situational and environmental conditions that encourage destruction, not the least of which include the institutional characteristics of the schools and the influences of peers. The *Safe School Study* (1977) made a valuable contribution to the field in investigating a number of within-school characteristics affecting property destruction. One-half to one-third of the variation in vandalism was accounted for by a small number of factors: the size and impersonal nature of the schools, the perceived arbitrary distribution of rewards and punishments, the relevance of activities and curriculum, academic emphasis, the general sense of student alienation, and students' perceptions of the legitimacy of vandalism as a response to the schools. The case studies portion of the NIE study showed that the key ingredients differentiating vandalized from non-vandalized schools included community involvement in the schools, a principal who could rally the support and cooperation of teachers, consistent and certain application of school rules, and the orderly structure of the school's routine.

Although the *Safe School Study* and other pieces of research indicate that community-crime rates and other factors influence vandalism, they also conclude that variables within the school appear to influence it still more. These school-specific variables can be changed. The problem can be addressed, and we are learning more about how to do it. What is needed, however, is the determination to understand the basic factors causing vandalism in any school setting, to create rational and efficient educational and security programs to address the basic causes, and the courage and determination to follow through. We hope that this book has contributed to this effect, and to the flowering of teaching and learning that must follow.

Appendix A
Resource Guide

This section is, of necessity, an incomplete listing of resources available to those wanting to reduce vandalism. A comprehensive guide would have been unpardonably long. The intent of this Resource Guide is to provide one with a starting point. A helpful hint in the search for resources might be simply stated: "Look at everyone and everything that comes along as a resource."

Students are an important resource, as are their parents. A brief check on the employment of parents, for instance, may afford you the opportunity for a guest speaker, or a program manager, or a field trip for students. Students and parents have taught minicourses and run projects. In addition, parents belong to groups, agencies, and clubs, and can be very helpful if you need expertise or simply a little understanding.

The list that follows presents some of the resources available to you while developing your program. Resource categories overlap: we suggest you look through all of them.

Alternative Education

Directory of Alternative Public Schools. Available through: Center for Options in Public Education; School of Education; Room 339; Indiana University; Bloomington, Indiana, 47401.

The directory contains exactly what its title states. The Center for Options in Public Education also has a number of other resources that are useful to those thinking of developing alternative-education programs.

Alternative Programs: A Grapevine Survey. Available from: U.S. Department of Commerce; National Technical Information Service; 5285 Port Royal Road; Springfield, Virginia (PB-229-728).

This National Council on Crime and Delinquency report presents a survey and discussion of alternative-education programs.

Alternatives to Suspension. Available from: South Carolina Community Relations Program; American Friends Service Committee; 301 Columbia Building; Columbia, South Carolina, 29201. Price: $1.00.

This 32-page handbook presents a number of options for schools in disciplining students. It includes information on such things as behavior contracts, alternative schools, suspension centers, cool-off rooms, peer counseling, and parent involvement.

Community and Parental Involvement

Gall, J. and Bullock, J. *Setting Goals for Your School District: A Community Involvement Guide for Educators.* Available through the Consortium for the Improvement of Professional Education; Eugene, Oregon, or through ERIC (ED151983).

The first section of this 83-page monograph explains the rationale for community involvement in schools, the second details the goal-setting process.

Helping Hand Program Kit. Available through: Citizens Forum, Inc.; 2735 North Illinois Street; Indianapolis, Indiana, 46208. Price: $25.

This kit contains resources and materials for implementing a block-watch program.

Behavior Change and Discipline

Rutherford and Swist, *Behavior Modifications with Juvenile Delinquents: Bibliography* 1973 (ED 094 296): Available at most local university libraries or through the ERIC Clearinghouse. Price: $1.50

This ERIC document contains a lengthy bibliography on research and programs using behavior-modification techniques with disruptive students.

Student Rights and School Discipline: Bibliography. Available through: Project for the Fair Administration of Student Discipline; The University of Michigan; Ann Arbor, Michigan.

Included is an annotated bibliography of available materials, laws, and papers on school discipline, student rights, and other related topics.

Benton, A. *Dissent and Disruption in the Schools: A Handbook for School Administrators 1971.* Available from: Institute for Development of Educational Activities, Inc.; Dayton, Ohio.

This handbook was written for school administrators to help them defuse tense situations that could lead to violence in the schools. It suggests tactical interventions and their moral and legal implications.

Discipline and Control Update December, 1976. Available from: CROFT-NEI Publications; 24 Rope Ferry Road; Waterford, Connecticut, 06386.

The Discipline and Control Update is published 12 times annually by CROFT-NEI. The December, 1976 edition contains tips on the use of custodians in vandalism projects. It also described a work program for identified vandals.

Discipline Crisis in the Schools: The Problem, Causes and Search for Solutions.
Available from: National School Public Relations Association; 1801 North
Moore; Arlington, Virginia, 22209

This Education U.S.A. Report presents an overview of discipline problems in
the nation's schools, and some suggestions for local-school administrators.

Howard, E. *School Discipline Desk Book.* Available from: Parker Publishing
Company; West Nyach, New York ($13.95) or through ERIC (ED150-707).

This 250-page handbook lists numerous suggestions for handling school-
discipline problems. Topics include how to conduct school anticrime cam-
paigns, helping teachers handle discipline problems, increasing student involvement in school activities, and modifying the curriculum. Two case studies
and an annotated bibliography are included.

Building Security, Design, and Target Hardening

Zeisel, J. *Stopping School Property Damage.* American Association of
School Administrators. 1801 North Moore Street; Arlington, Virginia, 22209.
Price $4.95.

This is probably the most comprehensive set of guidelines for reducing property
damage yet published. It contains a detailed list—with illustrations—of inexpensive design options for reducing nonmalicious vandalism.

Carlton, S.A. "Security Notebook: Surveying School Security and Costs."
Available in *Security World* 11 (1974):26-27, 46.

This article appearing in a 1974 edition of *Security World* provides guidance
for developing a local-school-security system.

Coppola, J.B. *An Orientation and Training Program for Security Officers in
an Urban High School.* Available through: Nova University; Fort Lauderdale,
Florida, 33314.

A doctoral dissertation presenting information and materials used in an eight-
month orientation and training program designed for school-security officials.

Burglar Alarm Design: USMES Teacher's Resource Book, 1973. Available
through the Educational Development Center; Newton, Massachusetts or from
ERIC (ED142-378).

A curriculum guide stressing school safety but challenging students in shop
to build their own burglar alarms.

Schoolhouse: Designing Schools to Minimize Damage from Vandalism and Normal Rough Play. Available from: Educational Facilities Laboratories, Inc.; 477 Madison Avenue; New York, New York, 10022.

This easy-to-read guide was written for school officials wanting to cut down on damage resulting from accidents and normal youthful exuberance. It contains a list of suggestions on inexpensive ways to reduce accidental property destruction.

Vandalism and Violence: Innovative Strategies Reduce Cost to Schools. Available from: National School Public Relations Association; 1801 North Moore; Arlington, Virginia, 22209.

A report summarizing some research and experimental programs designed to reduce vandalism and violence in schools. It contains a number of suggestions for reducing property damage.

Security in the Schools: Tips for Guarding the Safety of Teachers and Students. Available from: the United Federation of Teachers; New York, New York.

This illustrated booklet was written especially for New York teachers, but should be useful to all. The booklet contains very specific suggestions on individual precautions and tips on general security matters.

Vestermark, S. and Blauvelt, P. *Controlling Crime in Schools: A Handbook for School Administrators.* Englewood Cliffs, N.J.: Prentice Hall, 1978.

This 354-page handbook for school administrators at the building and central office levels was prepared by security officials in Prince George's County, Maryland. The book shows how to develop a security program, respond to various security problems, and maintain current programs. A special section on how to involve students is included.

Violence in Our Schools: What to Know about It, What to Do about It. Available through: National Committee for Citizens in Education; Wilde Lake Village Green; Suite 410; Columbia, Maryland, 21044. Call (800) NET-WORK.

This brochure was published specifically for parents wanting to help reduce violence in the schools. It contains information on how to get involved, on training, discipline, the law, and family educational rights.

Redmond, J. *Personnel Security Officer's Manual 1968.* Available from: Chicago Board of Education; 228 North LaSalle Street; Chicago, Illinois, 60601.

This manual provides training information for off-duty policemen working as school-security officers.

Redmond, J. *School Security Manual 1969.* Available from: Chicago Board of Education; 228 North LaSalle Street; Chicago, Illinois, 60601.

This manual contains a guide for school administrators with legal prescriptions for school security and information on what to do if security rules are broken.

Edgar, J. and King, R. *Crime and School Security: NCJRS Bibliography.* Available from: National Criminal Justice Reference Service; LEAA; Washington, D.C.

A lengthy annotated bibliography that contains references on school-security measures.

Baughman, P. *Vandalism and Its Prevention.* Available through: California Association of School Business Officials; 4100 Normal Street; San Diego, California, 92103, or ERIC (ED 091 829). Price: $2.06.

This report gives an overview of the vandalism problem and offers some suggestions on how to control losses from arson and other fires.

Coursen, D. *Vandalism Prevention.* Available from: National Association of Elementary School Principals; 1801 North Moore; Rosslyn, Virginia, 22209; or ERIC (Ed 111 051). Price: $1.50.

A 26-page report pulling together much of the available information on vandalism prevention. It contains, among other things, an inventory of types of equipment that are available to reduce vandalism.

References on Vandalism and Security Systems in Public Schools. Available from: Publications Department; National Education Association; 1201 16th Street, N.W.; Washington, D.C.

A list of references on security and hardware systems for schools.

Curricula and Films

Reutter, E. *The Courts and Student Conduct.* Available through: National Organization on Legal Problems of Education; 825 Western Avenue; Topeka, Kansas, 66606; or through ERIC (EA 006 406).

Not a curriculum package as such, but a detailed explanation of the law and how it applies to the schools. The piece covers recent Supreme Court rulings and how they relate to student discipline, due process, publications, dress and appearance, secret societies, marriage and parenthood, and student conduct. It is a thorough document and meant for school administrators and board members.

Violence and Vandalism: Current Trend in School Policies and Programs. Available from: National School Public Relations Association; 1801 North Moore; Arlington, Virginia, 22209.

This readable and attractive Education USA Report summarizes and describes dozens of violence and vandalism programs in schools across the country. It contains numerous suggestions for reducing vandalism.

Student Security Aide Manual. Available from: Pittsburgh Board of Public Education; 341 South Bellefield Avenue; Pittsburgh, Pennsylvania, 15213.

An 8-page manual offering suggestions and guidance for students who are working as security aides.

Reslock, C. *Manual on Property Protection.* Available from: Security Section, Administrative Services Branch; Los Angeles Unified School District; P.O. Box 3307 Terminal Annex; Los Angeles, California, 90051.

This handbook provides school administrators with legal information concerning security measures. It offers suggestions on protecting the buildings and on dealing with security violations.

School Disruptions: Tips for Educators and Police. Available from the Community Relations Service; U.S. Department of Justice; Washington, D.C.

This brochure has two sections: Preventing Disruptions and Responding to Disruptions. Each section has two parts: what schools should do and what police should do. The brochure outlines the basic steps school and police officials should take in developing a joint approach to school disruptions. Easy to use checklists are provided.

It's Your Right: The Law Says... Available through: National Education Association; 1201 16th St., N.W.; Washington, D.C.

This color filmstrip was designed for classroom use, and discusses individual rights under the law. The filmclip comes with a record narration and a discussion-leaders guide.

Violence and Vandalism Available from: American Educational Film Depository; 132 Lasky Drive; Beverly Hills, California, 90212.

A sixteen-minute film which comes in 16 mm, 8 mm, and video-cassette. The film, featuring Hugh O'Brian as the narrator, discusses causes and possible solutions to inner-city and suburban violence and vandalism.

Vandals. Available from: Walt Disney Film Depository; 11 Quine Street; Cranford, New Jersey, 07016

A seventeen-minute, Angie Dickinson narrated, film which traces what happens to two teenagers who are caught vandalizing their school. The film breaks at specific point to allow classroom discussion.

The Vandals. Available from: Xerox Films; ABC News; New York.

This twenty-four-minute film shows how vandalism and property destruction affects the quality of life.

Youth and the Administration of Justice. Available from: Constitutional Rights Foundation; Dade County, Florida.

This booklet summarizes the results of a Dade County education program. It also contains a great deal of information to help start your own program. This is one of the most complete booklets published.

Your Child and the Law. Available through: National Education Association; 1201 16th Street, N.W.; Washington, D.C.

A packet of thirty booklets and pamphlets written for parents whose children have trouble with the law. The package includes information on how to find a lawyer and how to give emotional support. There is also a state-by-state summary of penalties for drug possession.

Juvenile Justice: A High School Curriculum Guide. Available through: Institute for Political and Legal Education; P.O. Box 426; Pitman, New Jersey, 08071. Price: $5.00.

An experimental curriculum package developed for and tested in several New Jersey secondary schools. The package is complete with materials and instructions for use in classrooms. Areas covered include the courts, school law, school rights and responsibilities, arrests, and delinquency. Classroom exercises are included.

Vandalism: The Price is High. Available from: Law-Related Education Program; 2644 Riva Road; Annapolis, Maryland.

This curriculum guide and forty-five minute slide-show presentation was designed for teachers teaching a special course on school vandalism. The guide includes workbooks for students. This is one of the most complete and innovative course curricula.

Boy Who Liked Deer. Available through: Learning Corporation of America; 1350 Avenue of the Americas; N.Y., N.Y., 10019.

This nineteen-minute 16 mm color film is designed for elementary-school children and shows how one boy begins to realize the effects of damaging property.

More Than Just a Place to Come. Available through: Mitchell Gebhart Film Company; 1380 Bush Street; San Francisco, Calif., 94109.

This twenty-minute 16 mm color film shows interviews with student, parents, police, and school staff around a murder and fire in a local school.

Project Pride. Available through: Visucom Productions; P.O. Box 3563; Stanford, Calif., 94305.

This seventeen-minute film is designed for elementary-school administrators and shows ways to involve students in taking pride in their school.

Respect for Property. Available through: Coronet Instructional Films; 65 East South Water Street; Chicago, Ill., 60601.

This eleven-minute black-and-white film shows how a policeman teaches a group of boys to respect property after their clubhouse is burglarized.

Solutions to Vandalism. Available through: Harper and Row Media; 2350 Virginia Ave.; Hagerstown, Md., 21740

This thirty-five-minute film shows six differing communities and how they worked to confront vandalism and violence.

Take a Little Pride. Available through: Visucom Productions; P.O. Box 3563; Stanford, Calif., 94305.

This ten-minute 16 mm film is another in a series on school-pride programs designed for elementary-school youngsters.

Vandalism. Available through: University of Minnesota; Audiovisual Library Service; Continuing Education and Extension.

This eleven-minute film bluntly shows the legal consequences of vandalism: jail.

The Clubhouse. Available through: Harper and Row Media; 2350 Virginia Ave.; Hagerstown, Md., 21740.

This ten-minute film is widely acclaimed for elementary-school children, showing from a child's perspective how vandalism feels when one is the victim.

Why Vandalism. Available through: Encyclopedia Britannica; Educational Corporation; 1150 Wilmette Ave.; Wilmette, Ill., 60091.

This 1955 seventeen-minute film looks at the causes of vandalism for a personality perspective. A bit out of date.

Vandalism—Why? Available from: Perennial Education, Inc.; 1825 Willow Rd.; P.O. Box 236; Northfield, Ill., 60093. Price: $14 (rental); $140 (sale).

An eleven-minute 16 mm film discussing vandalism and the influences of peer groups and social pressure. Several suggestions for constructive projects are offered.

Facing Up to Vandalism. Available from: Perennial Education, Inc.; 1825 Willow Road; P.O. Box 236; Northfield, Ill., 60093. Price: $21 (rental): $210 (sale).

A sixteen-minute 16 mm film designed to stimulate classroom discussions. The film shows inner-city, suburban, and rural junior-high-school students talking about their involvement in vandalism.

Dealing with Aggressive Behavior: A Curriculum for Middle School and Junior High: Teachers Manual. Available from: Educational Research Council of America; Cleveland, Ohio.

This curriculum guide for teachers was developed for the Lakewood City, Ohio, Board of Education to help deal with disruptive students.

Human Race, and Community Relations

You Don't Have to Love Each Other But . . . Available through: American Institutes for Research; Cambridge, Mass. or from Hinds, Vladeck and Garrett, Inc.; 46 Morton Road; Newton Centre, Massachusetts.

This work is a guide for teachers, students, and parents who are involved in the desegregation process. It is ideal for use in the classroom or for informal-group-discussion sessions.

Pritchard, R. and Wedra, V. *Resource Manual for Reducing Conflict and Violence in California Schools.* Available from: California School Boards Association; 800 North Street; Sacramento, California, 95814.

This manual contains, among other things, annotations of some California counseling programs designed to reduce the level of crime and violence in the schools. The manual also includes a description of an interagency community approach to reducing conflict.

Olson, C. *Developing School Pride Reducing Vandalism: A Guide for Student Leaders.* Available from: San Diego City Department of Schools; 4100 Normal Street; San Diego, California, 92103.

The manual provides guidelines for student leaders for beginning student-antivandalism programs in schools.

Delinquency Today: A Guide for Community Action 1971 Available from: U.S. Government Printing Office; Washington, D.C.

This handbook presents advice on how to involve the community in reducing juvenile delinquency.

Quad '74. Available from: Office of the Attorney General, Crime Prevention Unit, ATTN: Quad '74; 3580 Wilshire Blvd.; 9th Floor; Los Angeles, California, 90010.

A directory of youth-service agencies and programs to prevent delinquency and vandalism. It was written for Southern California schools.

Solutions to Conflict and Violence in the Schools. Available from: Yerba Buena High School; East Side Union High School District; San Jose, California.

This booklet offers guidelines for setting up a coordinated community effort to reduce school vandalism.

School Vandalism: Program Strategies. Available from: The Council of the Great City Schools; 1707 H Street, N.W.; Washington, D.C., 20006.

This package forms the basis for this book.

Insurance

The Department of Housing and Urban Development operates an effort called the Federal Crime Insurance Program to insure schools, small commercial businesses, and residences against burglary and riots. Although burglary is covered under the policy, general property destruction is not. In addition, ask if your state participates in the Fair Plan. For information concerning eligibility, contact: Federal Insurance Administration; Department of Housing and Urban Development; Washington, D.C., 20410, (202) 755-6555.

Journals

A number of periodicals are published that routinely report on successful vandalism- and violence-prevention programs and on new techniques in the field. Most of these journals can be found either in hard or microfiche copies at the local college or university library. Much of the information gathered for this book came from these journals. It is a good idea to scan them period-ically for ideas:

1. *American School Board Journal*
2. *American School and University*
3. *Today's Education*
4. *Security World*

5. *Nation's Schools*
6. *NASSP Bulletin*
7. *School Product News*
8. *Phi Delta Kappan*

A look through the bibliography of this book can give you specific articles in each journal. Many contain very specific and practical suggestions for reducing vandalism.

Peer Counseling and Tutoring

Cross-Age Helping Program: Orientation, Training, and Related Materials. Available through: Institute for Social Research; University of Michigan; Ann Arbor, Michigan.

A collection of materials to aid in the development of a cross-age tutorial program for the fourth through eighth grades. Evaluation materials are included.

Klaus, D. *Patterns of Peer Tutoring.* Available through: American Institutes for Research; 1055 Thomas Jefferson Street, N.W.; Washington, D.C., 20007.

This work is both a literature review and a guide for teachers and administrators wanting to start a peer-tutoring program. It includes a discussion on how to avoid some common pitfalls.

Gartner, A.; Kohler, M.; and Riessman, F. *Children Teach Children: Learning by Teaching.* Available through: Harper & Row, Inc.; 49 E. 33rd Street; New York, New York, 10016.

Discusses some of the general procedures and instructions for setting up a peer-tutoring program.

Peer Counseling. Available from: Professional Information Services, Library, American Personnel and Guidance Association; 5203 Leesburg Pike; Falls Church, Va. 22041. Free.

A lengthy bibliography of references prepared by the major school-counselors' professional association.

A Cross-Age Teaching Resource Manual. Available through: La Verne College; La Verne, CA. Price: $3.00

A detailed description of one cross-age tutoring program in California. Special attention is given to how to train student tutors.

Harrison, G. *How to Organize an Intergrade Tutoring Program in an Elementary School.* Available through: Brigham Young University Printing Service; Salt Lake City, Utah. Price: 2.65.

The author explains how to set up a structured tutoring program using simple school-made materials.

Ebersole, E. *A Teachers Guide to Programmed Tutoring in Reading.* Available through: Eberson Enterprises; 120 W. Union Street; Pasadena, CA. Price: $3.95.

This report describes a peer-tutoring program at the Soto Street School in Los Angeles. It includes training and tutor materials.

Klausmeier, H. *Tutoring Can Be Fun.* Available through: Wisconsin Research and Development Center for Cognitive Learning; University of Wisconsin. Price: $1.75.

A booklet for upper-elementary and junior-high school tutors. It is fun to read whether or not you have a peer-tutoring program.

Program Evaluation

Hawkridge, D.; Campeau, P.; and Trickett, P. *Preparing Evaluation Reports: A Guide for Authors.* Available through: U.S. Office of Education; Information Materials Center; 400 Maryland Ave., S.W.; Washington, D.C., 20202. Price: $1.25.

This is an easy-to-read guide for school people on how to conduct and write evaluations. It also contains a list of references for those who have little background in program evaluation.

Mager, R. *Preparing Instructional Objectives.* Available through: Fearon Publishers; 6 Davis Drive; Belmont, Calif., 94002. Price: $2.00.

This small book is useful to those wanting to set objectives and measurable goals for their school programs.

Ideabook. Available through the National Joint Dissemination Review Panel; National Institute of Education; Washington, D.C. Free.

This short booklet spells out the evaluation criteria that the JDRP uses in deciding on which federally sponsored programs to consider exemplary.

Rights and Responsibilities

Emerging Rights of Students: The Minnesota Model for a Student Bill of Rights. Available through: National School Public Relations Association; 1801 North Moore Street; Arlington, VA, 22209.

This handbook contains Minnesota's concept of a school rights-and-responsibilities code. It contains guidance on alcohol, drugs, appearance, pregnancy, smoking, student records, and many other topics.

Model High School Disciplinary Procedure Code. Available through: National Juvenile Law Center; 3642 Lindell Blvd.; St. Louis, Missouri, 63108.

NJLC's version of a model rights codes.

A Model Student Code. Available through: Phi Delta Kappa; 8th and Union; Bloomington, Indiana, 47401.

This is PDK's version of an ideal student-rights code. It includes information on suspensions, equal educational opportunity, student searches, involuntary classification, and other areas.

Ackerly, R. *The Reasonable Exercise of Authority.* Available through: The National Association of Secondary School Principals; 1201 16th Street, N.W.; Washington, D.C., 20036.

A short 28-page booklet that interprets for school principals the implications of recent Supreme Court rulings on various student rights.

Suspensions and Due Process: An Analysis of Recent Supreme Court Decisions on Student Rights. Available through: Robert F. Kennedy Memorial; 1035 30th Street, N.W.; Washington, D.C., 2007.

This booklet was prepared for students, parents, and community members to help them understand the implications of recent Supreme Court rulings.

What Every Teacher Should Know about Student Rights. Available through: National Education Association; 1201 16th Street, N.W.; Washington, D.C., 20036.

It explains for teachers their rights and also the rights of students. It includes information on punishment, discrimination, grades, and other areas.

The Rights of Students. Available through: Avon Books; 250 W. 55th Street; New York, New York, 10019. Price: $.95.

Published by the ACLU, this booklet is probably the best overall resource on student rights. The ACLU also publishes a similar work for teachers.

Students' Rights: A Guide to the Rights of Children, Youth, and Future Teachers. Available through: Association of Teacher Educators; 1701 K Street, N.W.; Washington, D.C.

This manual was designed for inservice student teachers.

Model Code of Student Rights and Responsibilities. Available through: Center for Law and Education; Cambridge, Mass., 02138.

This is another model code for students rights. It presents information on due process, freedom of expression, right to education, religious expression, and other topics.

The Rights and Responsibilities of Public School Students in Michigan. Available through: Saginaw Student Rights Center; 1407 James Street; Saginaw, Michigan, 49601.

Michigan's official student rights and responsibilities are laid out in this booklet.

Code of Student Rights and Responsibilities. Available through: National Education Association; 1201 16th Street; N.W., Washington, D.C.

Another one of NEA's numerous works on student and teacher rights and responsibilities in schools.

From the American Bar Association, Special Committee on Youth Education; 1155 East 60th Street; Chicago, Illinois, 60637, come the following:

Catalogue of law-related audio-visual materials.

Bibliography of law-related curriculum materials.

Directory of law-related educational activities. Price: $2.00.

The $$ Game: A guidebook on the funding of law-related educational programs.

All these resources provide an excellent starting point for developing and implementing a law-education program in your schools. The directory describes over 170 law-related education programs for elementary and secondary students.

The recently passed Education Amendments of 1978 authorizes discretionary monies for the secretary to support new law-related and corrections educational programs in the schools. The amendments also authorize funds for safe schools projects. To date the money for both have been limited to nonexistent.

Technical Assistance

LEAA has awarded a $2.5 million grant to the Center for Human Services to establish a National School Resource Center and a series of regional centers. The program is now in operation and is designed to provide technical assistance, training, and curricular services. For further information, call (202) 654-2550 or write to the Center at 5530 Wisconsin Avenue, N.W.; Washington, D.C., 20015.

Appendix B
Sample Security/
Vandalism Report
Forms: General

Vandalism Incident Form

		Elementary Schools		Secondary Schools		Totals
		School A	School B	School D	School E	
Graffiti	# $					
Glass Breakage	# $					
Theft or larceny	# $					
Breaking & Entering	# $					
Bombings & Bomb Threats	# $					
Littering	# $					
Mechanical or Non-deliberate fires	# $					
Automobile Damage	# $					
Property Damage	# $					
Property Defacing	# $					
Burglary	# $					
Arson	# $					
Totals	# $					

Target-Hardening Security Checklist

School _____   Date _____

Address _____   Grade Level _____

Contact _____   District _____

Play Areas

1. What have you done to minimize breakage in playgrounds and basket-ball courts?

	Yes	No
There is sufficient space around formal play areas for normal play	___	___
Ground surfaces in and around formal play areas have no major irregularities or hindrances to play	___	___
Wall surfaces around formal play areas can be used to bounce balls back to players	___	___
Low lighting fixtures and other hardware are out of the way of ball playing	___	___
Lines on walls and on ground accommodate local street games	___	___
There is a buffer between formal play areas and the school building	___	___
There are no windows or glass doors around formal play areas	___	___
Glass around formal play areas is specially protected	___	___
There is no damageable planting immediately adjacent to formal play areas	___	___

2. What have you done to assure that objects will not be broken in play areas?

	Yes	No
There are consciously designed areas for pickup play	___	___
There is no low lighting or other fixtures which can be hit by balls in pick-up play areas	___	___

This checklist is a revised version of one published by the American Association of School Administrators in an excellent booklet, *Stopping School Property Damage*. Reprinted with permission.

	Yes	No

Walls and ground surfaces in pick-up play areas are the
same as in formal play areas   ____ ____

There are no windows in pick-up play areas   ____ ____

Any windows near pick-up play areas are protected
from balls and sticks   ____ ____

3. What have you done to assure that playground equipment can with-
    stand rough treatment?

Playground equipment needs special tools to be
disassembled   ____ ____

Official play equipment can accommodate extra rough
play by groups sometimes older than those for whom
equipment is officially specified   ____ ____

Informal Gathering Spots

1. What have you done to minimize damage in niches, small doorways
    and corners?

There are no niches around doorways, under stairways,
or other places within the school   ____ ____

Where there are niches within the school, these are
necessary for reasons of safety   ____ ____

There are no fixtures, windows, or door glass in neces-
sary niches   ____ ____

Walls in necessary niches are tiled or painted with
epoxy paint   ____ ____

Ceilings in necessary niches are solid   ____ ____

2. What have you done to minimize damage in places where students gather
    to talk?

There are some consciously planned student gathering
areas in the school, and these are durable enough to
take rough use.   ____ ____

Walls in gathering areas are painted with epoxy paint   ____ ____

Walls in gathering areas are covered with glazed tile   ____ ____

	Yes	No
Some walls in gathering areas are lighter than other walls and have blocked-out surfaces in order to attract and thereby channel graffiti	___	___
There are no fixtures or hardware in gathering areas	___	___
Fixtures and hardware in gathering areas are out of reach of students	___	___
Fixtures within reach of students in gathering areas are extra durable	___	___
Equipment in gathering areas likely to be used as a bench is reinforced and made extra durable	___	___
There are no glass and no windows in potential gathering areas	___	___
There is no glass in gathering areas which is lower than three feet from the floor	___	___
There are trash containers in potential gathering areas	___	___
There are alternative legitimate lounges for students to use as an alternative to informal gathering areas	___	___
Legitimate student lounges are not visible from offices or classrooms and are accessible without having to pass through such places	___	___
There are legitimate ways for students to personalize gathering areas, for example, on graffiti-receptive wood or painted walls	___	___

3. What have you done to assure that students have places to hang out informally which are damage-free?

	Yes	No
Hang-out areas are consciously identified and prepared for heavy use	___	___
There are no wall fixtures located in hang-out areas	___	___
There are some wall fixtures in hang-out areas, but these are out of reach of two teenages one on the other's shoulders or one with a stick	___	___
Fixtures within reach in hang-out areas are extra durable	___	___

	Yes	No
There are convenient and durable trash containers in hang-out areas	___	___
There are consciously planned places to sit in hang-out areas	___	___
Fixtures and ledges in hang-out areas which might be sat upon by groups of students are durable enough for this use	___	___
Fixtures and hardware on hang-out area walls and ceilings which might be hung upon or climbed upon have reinforced attachments	___	___
Both formal and informal sitting places in hang-out areas are far from breakable windows and equipment	___	___
There are some walls in hang-out areas which are lighter and more evenly scored than other walls, and which can be predicted to attract graffiti	___	___
There is a formally identified graffiti board in hang-out areas	___	___

4. What have you done to minimize damage in outdoor areas where students gather informally?

	Yes	No
There are consciously designed and located areas for hanging out	___	___
There are no fixtures in or near hang-out areas	___	___
All fixtures in hang-out areas have tamper-proof screws	___	___
All hardware and fixtures in hang-out areas are extra durable	___	___
There are no windows in or nearby hang-out areas	___	___
Windows in hang-out areas are specially protected	___	___
Planting in hang-out areas bends easily and grows quickly	___	___
There is no stiff and breakable planting in hang-out areas	___	___
There are benches or steps or ledges for sitting in hang-out areas	___	___

	Yes	No
All predicted sitting places in hang-out areas are far from breakable windows and fixtures	—	—
Low walls, ledges, and steps in hang-out areas are made of extra durable material	—	—
There are heavy trash containers in hang-out areas	—	—
Trash containers in hang-out areas are designed to seem like targets for litter	—	—
There are no planters in hang-out areas which can be used as trash baskets	—	—
Replacements for small unit building materials used in hang-out areas, like bricks or panels can be easily stored	—	—

5. What have you done to minimize damage to outdoor shrubbery?

	Yes	No
Near active areas, all planting is flexible, resilient, and pliable	—	—
There is no thorny planting to collect litter and prevent cleaning	—	—
There is no thick planting which will be difficult to clean around	—	—
There is no climbable planting near edge of buildings	—	—
There is no planting in predictable pick-up, play and hang-out, nor in gathering areas	—	—

Indoor Facilities

1. What have you done to minimize damage in lavatories

	Yes	No
There are no exposed plumbing pipes	—	—
There are no exposed bathroom accessories	—	—
Bathroom fixtures can be easily and inexpensively repaired if damaged	—	—
Air vents are located so they cannot easily be used as ashtrays	—	—
Wastepaper baskets are of a type which will not be permanently damaged if used as ashtrays	—	—

	Yes	No
Walls, up to the ceiling, are covered with heavy duty material	___	___
Floors in lavatories are extra durable	___	___
Ceilings in lavatories are solid	___	___
Ceiling elements in lavatories are specially designed to withstand poking with a stick	___	___
Vertical elements holding up toilet partitions are attached to structural members in floor and ceiling	___	___
Toilet partitions have tamper-proof screws	___	___
Toilet partitions can be easily painted without looking shoddy	___	___
There is some formally identified place in lavatories on which students can legitimately write—wood plank, painted wall, chalkboard	___	___
There are consciously designed private social places for students, other than the lavatory	___	___
There are durable benches in alternative social places for students	___	___

2. What have you done to minimize graffiti?

	Yes	No
There are some walls for possible graffiti which are lighter than other walls and have blocked out sections in watering holes, hang-out areas, and entry ways	___	___
There are some formally labeled "graffiti boards" in high-use public areas	___	___
There are some consciously designed informal graffiti walls which have easily and inexpensively cleaned or painted surfaces	___	___
Walls on which graffiti is to be discouraged have inexpensively and easily cleaned or painted surfaces	___	___
Informal and formal graffiti walls have surfaces on which sections can be selectively cleaned	___	___

                                                                    Yes · No

3. What have you done to minimize damage in cafeterias?

    There are trash receptacles at the ends of each row of
    tables in the cafeteria   ____ ____

    Cafeteria furniture cannot be disassembled with
    conventional hand tools   ____ ____

4. What have you done to minimize damage to shop equipment?

    There is a central locked storage area large enough for
    all hand tools   ____ ____

5. What have you done to minimize damage to doors?

    All doors which are primarily exit doors have no locks
    or door handles   ____ ____

    Where there is a series of connected doors, only one
    of these doors have exterior door hardware   ____ ____

    There are no glass or other transparent panels on doors
    which give a clear view of panic hardware   ____ ____

    There are astragals on all shingle doors   ____ ____

    Double doors are extra duty strength   ____ ____

    Double doors have sturdy center mullions   ____ ____

    Double doors have astragals   ____ ____

    Panic hardware require minimum amount of mechan-
    ical movement   ____ ____

    Panic hardware is easily repaired   ____ ____

    There are large sliding grills or garage type doors to
    cover transparent doorways in the entrance and are
    visible from a distance when school is closed   ____ ____

    Deep recesses at entries are inaccessible when school
    is closed   ____ ____

    The entry way looks open when school is open but
    closed when school is closed   ____ ____

	Yes	No
Door knobs and door closures are specified to withstand especially rough use	___	___
Door closures cannot be disassembled with ordinary hand tools	___	___
Built-in door hardware can be easily repaired if damaged	___	___

6. What have you done to minimize window and glass breakage?

	Yes	No
There are no windows in formal play areas	___	___
There are no windows in informal gathering areas	___	___
In vulnerable areas windows are made of several small panes, rather than one large pane	___	___
There are no windows lower than three feet from the ground	___	___
There is no acrylic or plexiglass in windows in watering holes and hang-out areas	___	___
Windows on higher floors are of decreasing strength	___	___
Windows adjacent to interior watering holes or hang-out areas on upper floors, as well as on the ground, are especially durable	___	___
There is extra thick tempered glass or double layer glass where acrylic or plexiglass is not advisable	___	___
There are no windows at all in student stores	___	___
There are no windows at all in administration storage offices	___	___
There are no windows at all in industrial arts storage areas	___	___
There are thin wire mesh screens over specially vulnerable ground floor windows	___	___
Ground floor windows are made of extra thick tempered glass	___	___
Ground floor windows are made of thick acrylic or plexiglass	___	___

	Yes	No
Ground floor windows are covered with protective screens	—	—

7. What have you done to minimize damage to fixtures?

	Yes	No
There are no fixtures on otherwise blank walls	—	—
Highly visible fixtures on otherwise blank walls are covered by extra heavy grills	—	—
All fixtures are out of reach of kids on each others' shoulders or holding sticks	—	—
All fixtures are higher than ground level where they can be kicked or stood on	—	—
There are no unnecessary fixtures on building exterior	—	—
All fixtures are recessed	—	—
All fixtures are covered with heavy duty protective plate	—	—
There are no vulnerable rainwater pipes below 6 feet from the ground	—	—
There are no lighting fixtures with plastic covers	—	—
Lighting fixtures are covered with armor-place glass	—	—
Site fixtures are able to be climbed on and used as targets	—	—
Site fixtures do not challenge students to damage them	—	—
All fixtures or equipment which protrude from walls are extra heavy duty	—	—
There are no hardware or fixtures which can be climbed upon or played with in informal gathering or formal play areas	—	—
All equipment has tamper-proof screws	—	—
Light fixtures are located out of reach of kids on each other's shoulders or carrying sticks	—	—
Light fixtures are recessed	—	—
Thermostats are located out of reach of passing students	—	—

	Yes	No
Thermostats are recessed	–––	–––
Air conditioners are placed out of view on inaccessible part of the roof	–––	–––
Fixtures and hardware do not make loud sounds when hit, touched or damaged	–––	–––
When damaged, fixtures and hardware do not remain in one piece providing students with a trophy	–––	–––

8. What have you done to minimize damage in gymnasiums and auditoriums?

	Yes	No
Design of auditorium takes into account special informal uses as well as standard activities	–––	–––
Auditorium seating is comfortable but does not offer materials to play with like string, buttons, knobs, or leather	–––	–––
Auditorium seating is assembled with tamper-proof screws or sunken bolts	–––	–––
Walls as high as can be reached in auditorium are painted with epoxy paint or tiled	–––	–––
Fixtures around the stage, especially at foot level or along the stage skirt are especially durable	–––	–––
All control boxes are covered with heavy duty lockable grilles	–––	–––
Fixtures in auditorium are located out of reach of kids standing on seats or armrests	–––	–––
There are large uncluttered walls in the gymnasium for impromptu ball playing	–––	–––
There are no wall fixtures within reach of people sitting on the bleachers	–––	–––
Wall fixtures in the gymnasium are located in corners or on side walls out of the way of stray balls	–––	–––
There are no clocks behind the basketball backboard	–––	–––
Equipment storage lockers are visible to permanent staff offices	–––	–––

	Yes	No
Gymnasium floor surface can stand up to nonsport uses involving contact with tables, chairs, and walking shoes	___	___
If gym floors requiring special maintenance are installed, commitments have been secured for ongoing maintenance training programs	___	___

9. What have you done to minimize damage to ceilings, floors and rooftops?

	Yes	No
There are hard surfaced ceilings in lavatories, watering holes, and hang-out areas	___	___
There are no drop-in ceilings in lavatories watering holes, or hang-out areas	___	___
When drop-in ceilings are used, these are firmly attached, heavy ceiling tiles that give way only slightly under pressure	___	___
Ceilings are painted with epoxy paint	___	___
Paint on ceilings is the same color as the subsurface	___	___
Paint on ceilings is quick-drying	___	___
Carpeting is installed in small squares or other easily replaced units	___	___
All floor material can be repaired easily and quickly if damage occurs	___	___
There are hard surface floors where rough or dirty activity will be taking place	___	___
In quiet areas, there are soft surface floors	___	___
There are no carpets in arts and crafts areas, in snack areas, or near sinks or easels in classrooms	___	___
Carpets specified for noise reduction in work areas are attached to walls instead of floors, or acoustical tile is used	___	___
Glass on accessible rooftops is ground-floor-type	___	___
Fixtures on accessible rooftops are ground floor type	___	___
Hardware on accessible rooftop is ground floor type	___	___

Yes   No

Doors on accessible rooftops have minimum exterior
hardware   ____ ____

Windows on accessible rooftops have no exterior
hardware   ____ ____

There is no climbable planting or planting which will
grow to be climbable located near building walls   ____ ____

There are no built-in footholds on telephone poles
adjacent to the building   ____ ____

Walls are too high to be climbed with 12 foot 2 x 4 or
other ladder substitute, i.e., wall is over 14 feet high   ____ ____

Fixtures on buildings do not provide footholds for
getting onto roofs   ____ ____

Incinerator and incinerator housing on roof cannot be
climbed upon or used to get from one roof to another   ____ ____

Gas meter cannot be climbed upon   ____ ____

Fixtures on rooftop walls cannot be used as footholds
for climbing to other parts of roof   ____ ____

Permanent custodian ladders are replaced by convenient
storage for portable ladders   ____ ____

Heights of roofs adjacent to rooftops accessible from
the ground are too high to be climbed with use of a
12-foot 2 x 4   ____ ____

10.   What have you done to minimize damage to walls?

Large expanses of walls are made of small wall sections
which can be individually repaired or replaced
inexpensively   ____ ____

Paint on walls is of a similar color to the substrate of
the wall material itself   ____ ____

In damage-prone areas, walls are made of harder
materials   ____ ____

Walls in highly traveled areas are covered with epoxy
paint or glazed tile   ____ ____

Paint used is quick drying   ____ ____

Property Control

		Yes	No

1. What have you done to inventory your equipment?

    All serialized equipment, e.g. office machines, lawn mowers, microscopes have been recorded and filed   ____   ____

    All nonserialized equipment has been counted   ____   ____

    Person has been assigned to make sure that all inventories are up to date   ____   ____

    All large equipment has the name of the school or some code painted or etched on it   ____   ____

    All material checked out from school buildings requires a signed receipt   ____   ____

    Access to storerooms is limited and clear key policy is in effect   ____   ____

    Storeroom locks have different keys from main door locks   ____   ____

    School money is always counted in secure location   ____   ____

    Vending machines are emptied each day   ____   ____

    Signs to storerooms have been removed   ____   ____

Security Program Audit

School _____ Date _____

Address _____ Grade Level _____

Contact _____ District _____

Security Personnel:

	Yes	No
Have you hired all the security personnel you originally intended?	——	——

Are the Security personnel you hired trained in

	Yes	No
a. Human relations	——	——
b. Police work	——	——
c. Operation of your security system	——	——
d. Administrative responsibilities	——	——
e. Student rights	——	——
f. Community outreach	——	——
g. Judicial process	——	——

	Yes	No
Are there indications that the presence of security personnel may irritate students or staff?	——	——
Are security personnel able to respond quickly to emergency alarms?	——	——
Does the security department have a clearly defined set of objectives and institutional responsibilities?	——	——
Does the security force have a high rate of absenteeism and/ or turnover?	——	——
Does the school maintain the authority to hire and fire security personnel?	——	——

Security Equipment

	Yes	No
Has your false alarm rate decreased over the last two years?	——	——
Does your equipment have a guarantee against failure or malfunction?	——	——
Have you done a cost analysis of the equipment in your schools?	——	——

	Yes	No
Is your equipment given a regular maintenance check?	___	___
Is there evidence that the presence of security equipment irritates students or staff?	___	___
Does your equipment adequately cover the areas and property of greatest risk in your buildings?	___	___
Is your equipment designed to address your most frequent type of property destruction?	___	___
Does your equipment have a high failure rate?	___	___
Are there indications that your equipment is easy to fool?	___	___
Have you systematically evaluated the efficacy of the security equipment in a sample of your schools?	___	___

Protective Measures

	Yes	No
Do you have formal procedures for handling keys?	___	___
Do you have specific policies for entry into school buildings?	___	___

Have you taken adequate precautions to lessen unintentional damage of:

	Yes	No
a. Bathrooms	___	___
b. Hallways	___	___
c. Walls	___	___
d. Windows	___	___
e. Books	___	___
f. Automobiles	___	___
g. Gymnasiums	___	___
h. Administration offices and classrooms	___	___
i. Buses	___	___

Community Involvement

	Yes	No
Have you included parents in the designing and running of the program?	___	___
Are teachers and staff permitted the opportunity to alter the security program?	___	___

	Yes	No

Do students participate in the program's operation and decision-making? ____ ____

Do parents and students receive training if they are involved in the program? ____ ____

Are various community groups, city agencies and businesses included in how the program is operated? ____ ____

Evaluation

Have you done a recent assessment of the nature of your vandalism problem? ____ ____

Is an evaluation component built into your program plan? ____ ____

Do you use the results of your evaluation data for decision-making? ____ ____

Do you have a clear set of objectives for your program? ____ ____

Staff Training

Have school staff been trained in the use of the security program? ____ ____

Have all staff been trained in their rights and responsibilities and those of the students? ____ ____

Appendix C
Security/Vandalism
Report Forms for
Specific Areas

Metropolitan Public Schools Building Inventory

CHECK LIST

DATE:_____

SCHOOL_____   GRADE LEVEL_____

ADDRESS_____   DISTRICT _____

A. ALARM

    1. Security:

        a. Manufacture _____   TYPE_____

        b. Monitored (How)_____

                _____

    2. Fire:

        a. Manufacture_____   TYPE_____

        b. Monitored (How) _____

                _____

B. LOCKS (DOOR)

    1. Number of Doors _____

    2. Type of Locking Devices _____

C. LOCKS (WINDOW)

    1. Number of accessible, first floor windows _____

    2. Type of Locks _____

    3. Types of Glass _____

    4. Screens: Yes _____   No_____

    5. Basement (window)

        a. Type of Locks _____

        b. Types of Glass _____

        c. Screens: Yes _____   No_____

D. **LIGHTS** (EXIT)

    1. Number of interior fire exit lights _____

E. **LIGHTS** (SECURITY)

    1. Number of Security Lights _____

        a. Type _____

        b. Candlepower _____

        c. Locations _____

F. **FIRE EQUIPMENT**

    1. Extinguishers: Number_____   Type _____

    2. Hose Cabinets: Number _____   Type _____

G. **SPRINKLER SYSTEM**

    1. How Fed: Mains_____   Tank_____   Pump_____   Reservoir_____

    2. Pressure **Highest** Sprinkler _____

    3. Location of Main Control Valve _____

    4. How Secured _____

    5. Amount of Floor Area Covered _____

    6. How Often and by Whom Inspected _____

        _____

    7. Flow Alarms? Yes_____   No_____

    8. Good Condition?   Yes_____   No_____ (if No, explain)_____

        _____

H. **HAZARDS** (LIST ALL)

    1. Fire_____

        _____

    2. Safety_____

        _____

    3. Security_____

        _____

I. SECURITY AREAS (LIST PROBLEMS)

    1. Administrative_____

    2. Sensitive Areas _____

J. FENCES

    1. Type_____

    2. Location (Coverage)_____

K. DATE OF SCHOOL CONSTRUCTION _____

L. TYPE OF CONSTRUCTION _____

COMMENTS:_____
_____
_____
_____
_____

Complaint Report

		COMPLAINT NO.
BALTIMORE CITY PUBLIC SCHOOLS SECURITY DIVISION	TYPE OF OFFENSE	

1. SCHOOL	2. DATE AND TIME OCCURRED	3. DATE AND TIME REPORTED	
4.COMPLAINANTS NAME (LAST, FIRST, MIDDLE)		5. COMPLAINANTS ADDRESS AND PHONE #	
6. COMPLAINANT'S SEX — RACE — AGE — DOB		7. LOCATION OF OFFENSE	
8. NATURE AND CONDITION OF INJURIES		9. WHERE TREATED	10. HOW TRANSPORTED

11. WEAPON OR MEANS OF ATTACK

13. IDENTIFY SUSPECTS BY NO. (NAME, ADDRESS, SEX, RACE, AGE, HT., WT., EYES, HAIR, COMPLEX., CLOTHING, IDENTIFYING CHARACTERISTICS.)

(1)

(2)

14. DESCRIPTION OF PROPERTY TAKEN (MAKE, MODEL, SERIAL #, COLOR, VALUE)

15. BALTIMORE CITY POLICE REPORT (DATE, TIME, OFFICER, DISTRICT)

ITEM NO.	16. NARRATIVE: (1) CONTINUATION OF ABOVE ITEMS (INDICATE "ITEM NUMBER" CONTINUED AT LEFT) INCLUDE ADDITIONAL VICTIMS, SUSPECTS AS OUTLINED ABOVE (2) DESCRIBE DETAILS OF INCIDENT. (3) DESCRIBE EVIDENCE AND PROPERTY AND INDICATE DISPOSITION.

17. REPORTING OFFICER	18. REVIEWING SUPERVISOR

Source: Baltimore City Public Schools, Baltimore, Maryland, Larry Burgam, Chief of Security. Reprinted with permission.

Principals' Report of Vandalism or Missing Property

(Control Number)

Pittsburgh Public Schools

_____
(To be filled by Security)

SECTION A:
School Name and Code _____ (___Code___) Report Date _____

Time of Incident: Date _____ Clock Time _____ ☐ A.M. ☐ P.M.

Loss or Vandalism Discovered By ☐ Custodian ☐ Security ☐ Administration ☐ Teacher ☐ Other

SECTION B: Break-in or Vandalism Point of Entry and Location of Vandalism	**SECTION D:** Damage To: ☐ Glass — Number of Panes, Type and Sizes

SECTION C: Type of Missing Equipment
☐ Audio Visual (Type, Make, Model and Serial Numbers)

☐ Affixed Equipment _____

☐ Electrical System _____

☐ Plumbing _____

☐ Office Machines or Equipment (Type, Make, Model and Serial Numbers)

☐ Landscaping _____

☐ Other _____

SECTION E: Additional Information on Missing Equipment:

☐ Musical Instruments (Kind, Make, Board Number Manufacturer's Serial Number)

1. Last Location Seen _____
2. Was Equipment Properly Stored? _____
   If Not Explain: _____
3. Could Equipment Be Observed From Outside of Classroom? _____ Was (were) Window(s) Locked?

☐ Other Types of Equipment (Type, Make, Model and Serial Numbers)

4. Was Classroom Locked? _____
   Was Cabinet or Storage Area Locked? _____
   If Not, Explain _____

- _If more space is needed, attach three (3) typed copies of additional information._
- _When Vandalism is indicated, and a B-65 is necessary, please attach one (1) copy of the Form B-65 to this report._
- _Retain School Copies—Forward all other copies to the Security Division._

☐ **THEFT**   ☐ **BREAK-IN**   ☐ **VANDALISM**   ☐ **LOST OR MISPLACED**

This report is not to reflect Personal Losses.

VANDALISM IS WILLFUL OR MALICIOUS DESTRUCTION OF PROPERTY

White Copy - Business Office
Yellow - Security Office
Pink - Line Supt.
Green - School Copy

_____
Signature of School Principal

Source: Pittsburgh Public Schools, Pittsburgh, Pennsylvania. Reprinted with permission.

Broward County, Florida, Property Incident Report

PLEASE FORWARD <u>FOUR</u> COPIES AS FOLLOWS:

WHITE	Maintenance & Operations Department	No._____
GREEN	Security Office	
GOLDENROD	Insurance Department	
BLUE	Property & Inventory	Date _____
PINK	School File	

> NOTE: Please list names of all suspects and/or witnesses on reverse side of GREEN COPY ONLY.

GENERAL INFORMATION
(Answer ALL Items)

SCHOOL _____

Date and time of incident _____

Was entry made into any part of the building?_____Which Police Dept. was called?_____

Custodial hours necessary to clean up? _____Name of investigator _____

Was Maintenance called? _____ Work Order Number assigned _____

_____ Willful damage _____Theft _____Carelessness   Other:_____

SPECIFIC DETAILS OF LOSS OR DAMAGE (Where, What, and How) _____

_____

_____

_____

_____

_____

_____

_____

MATERIAL AND EQUIPMENT STOLEN, DESTROYED, OR DAMAGED

No. of Items	NAME OF ITEM	DESCRIPTION (Model, Serial Number, etc.)	(CHECK ONE) Stolen	Destr.	Dam.	Purch. Year	Purchase Price

_____   _____
Person preparing report   Principal's Signature

BUS VANDALISM REPORT

School Bus No. _____ Bus Operator's Name _____

Type of Damage _____ Did incident occur on regular run?_____

To or from what school were students being transported? _____

_____   _____
Person preparing report   Principal's Signature

Source: The School Board of Broward County. Fort Lauderdale, Florida. Reprinted with permission.

Security Office Report, Grand Rapids School System

GRAND RAPIDS SCHOOL SYSTEM
GRAND RAPIDS, MICHIGAN

REPORT NO. _____

FILE CLASS _____

BUILDING OR DEPARTMENT CODE _____

TIME REPORTED _____DATE _____

REPORTED BY _____ADDRESS _____

POSITION _____ PHONE _____

NATURE OF INCIDENT_____

_____ ☐ ALARM

DATE AND TIME_____ ☐ DAMAGE   ☐ MISSING PROPERTY

AREA OCCURED_____

REPORT _____

_____

_____

_____

_____

_____

_____

_____

_____

_____

SUSPECTS.   ☐ NONE   ☐ APPREHENDED   ☐ KNOWN

1. _____

2. _____

3. _____

ITEMS MISSING — TYPE	BRAND	MODEL	CODE NO.	SERIAL NO.	VALUE
1.					
2.					
3.					
4.					
5.					
6.					

(USE BACK IF NEEDED)

REMARKS
OR
RECOM-
MENDATIONS: _____

_____

_____

_____

ACTION TAKEN: ☐ POLICE NOTIFIED. THEIR NO. _____   ☐ FILE CARDS MADE OUT _____

☐ OTHER_____   ☐ RECORDED _____

REPORT BY _____ TITLE _____

Source: Grand Rapids School System, Grand Rapids, Michigan. Reprinted with permission.

Prince George's County Public Schools
Security Incident Report and Self Insurance Form

			Police Number
	Area ☐ Northern ☐ Central ☐ Southern		Security Number

1. Complainant's Name	2. Title	3. Type of Incident	
4. Complainant's Address	5. Home Phone	6. Date Occurred	7. Time Occurred
8. City/State		9. Date Reported	10. Time Reported
11. Name of School	12. School Phone	13. Location of Incident	
14. Victim's Name	15. Race/Sex/DOB	16. Point of Entry	
17. Victim's Address	18. Home Phone	19. Means Used to Enter	
20. Victim's Condition	21. Parents Notified ☐ Yes ☐ No	22. Describe Weapon Used	

23. Description of Vehicle from which theft occurred. Year/Make/Model/Tag #

24. Suspect/Accused: Name/Address/Race/Sex/DOB/Hgt./Wgt./Hair/Type of haircut/scars/beard/Clothing

	25. Was Suspect Charged? ☐ Yes ☐ No	26. Student ☐ Yes ☐ No ☐ Unk	
27. School Property ☐ Yes ☐ No	28. Total Value of Property $	29. Personal Property ☐ Yes ☐ No	30. Value of Property $

31. Witness Name	Address	32. Home Phone	33. Business Phone
#1			
#2			

34. Police Notified ☐ Yes ☐ No	35. Officer's Name & Identification Number	36. Date Police Notified	37. Maint. Notified ☐ Yes ☐ No
38. Security Notified ☐ Yes ☐ No	39. Person Notified	40. Date Notified	41. Plant Oper. Not. ☐ Yes ☐ No
42. Bomb Threats/Arson: Bldg. Evac: ☐ Yes ☐ No	43. Fire Board Notification Name:	44. Time/Date	45. Did Fire Dept. Respond ☐ Yes ☐ No

46. NARRATIVE: Describe details of incident, include description of property lost, stolen or damaged, give value of each item, make, model and serial numbers, describe damage to building. (NOTE: if repairs to building are necessary submit a copy of this report to the Maintenance Dept.) Tell what action has been taken. Include in narrative a statement indicating what specific measures were taken to protect property lost or stolen.

(Use reverse side if additional space is required)

Principal's Signature	Date:

Form 10 M 3/76

Source: Prince George's County Public Schools, Upper Marlboro, Md. Reprinted with permission.

Pittsburgh Public Schools

OFFICE OF THE CHIEF OF SECURITY

REPORTED INCIDENTS IN SCHOOLS

WEEKLY GENERAL REPORT

SCHOOL _____   WEEK ENDING _____

OFFENSES

____ ATTACKS OR ASSAULTS ON SCHOOL EMPLOYEE

____ TEACHER

____ PARAPROFESSIONAL

____ OTHER _____ (Be Specific)

____ ATTACKS OR ASSAULTS ON SCHOOL EMPLOYEE BY:

____ STUDENT

____ PARENT, GUARDIAN

____ OTHER _____ (Be Specific)

____ ATTACKS OR ASSAULTS ON FELLOW STUDENTS

____ ATTACKS OR ASSAULTS ON FELLOW STUDENTS WITH WEAPONS

____ INTENTIONAL ACTS CAUSING SERIOUS BODILY INJURY TO A FELLOW STUDENT

____ SERIOUS FIGHTS BETWEEN STUDENTS

____ SERIOUS FIGHTS BETWEEN GROUPS OF STUDENTS

____ POSSESSION OF WEAPONS

OTHER OFFENSES

____ ALCOHOL

____ BOMB THREAT

____ DEMONSTRATION

____ DISORDERLY CONDUCT

____ EXTORTION

____ FALSE FIRE ALARM

____ FIRE

____ INTIMIDATION

____ NARCOTICS

____ LARCENY/ROBBERY/THEFT

____ SEX OFFENSE

____ TRESPASS

____ OTHER _____ (Be Specific)

ACTION TAKEN

____ ARRESTS

____ SUSPENSIONS

EXTENT OF INJURIES
(INCLUDING DRUG/NARCOTIC ABUSE)

____ MINOR, NO TREATMENT

____ TREATED AT SCENE

____ PERSONAL PHYSICIAN

____ HOSPITAL TREATMENT

____ REFUSED MEDICAL ATTENTION

_____
Signature of Person Filing Report/Title   Date

PLEASE FORWARD TO THE CHIEF OF SECURITY
SECURITY DIVISION, ADMINISTRATION BUILDING

Bibliography

The bibliography that follows contains those references cited throughout the book. It also contains other literature encountered in the course of working on this project. Although it is not comprehensive, the list should be useful for those conducting research or developing programs.

Abramson, P. 1972. AS&U's maintenance and operations cost study: property protection. *American School and University* 44:34-47.

Academy for Educational Development. 1972. *Need for immediate action.* New York: Academy for Educational Development.

Adams, V. 1970. What's behind rising insurance costs. *School Management* 14:27-33.

Aichhorn, A. 1931. *Wayward Youth.* New York: The Viking Press.

Allen, V. and Greenberger, D. 1978. An aesthetic theory of vandalism. *Crime and Delinquency* 24:309-321.

American Institutes for Research. 1975. *You don't have to love each other but.* Cambridge, Mass.

American Personnel and Guidance Association. 1977. *Report of American Personnel and Guidance Association Task Force on Juvenile Delinquency.* Washington, D.C.

American School Board Journal. 1972. Anatomy of a vandal and how one school district catches him. *American School Board Journal* 159:31.

_____. 1974. Another view: Let's get at the causes of youthful vandalism. *American School Board Journal* 161:68-69.

_____. 1974. Live-in 'school-sitters' are saving this district thousands of dollars each year—and cutting vandalism as well. *American School Board Journal* 161:36-38.

_____. 1974. Parent patrols are scaring would-be vandals away from schools in this burgeoning district. *American School Board Journal* 161:38-39.

_____. 1964. Protection & safety. *The American School Board Journal* 149:20-50.

_____. 1975. Violence in the schools: Everybody has solutions, and on the next ten pages, everybody offers them. *American School Board Journal* 162:27-37.

American School and University. 1973. A counterattack on vandalism. *American School and University* 45:43-44.

_____. 1974. Electronic security proves effective. *American School and University* 46:16.

_____. 1966. Lowering the toll of vandalism. *American School and University* 38:25-26.

———. 1970. 10 basic electronic security devices. *American School and University* 42:25-26.

———. 1974. School designed to shrug off vandalism. *American School and University* 47:28-30.

———. 1966. School security systems for maximum protection. *American School and University* 38:23-25.

———. 1971. To catch a thief, try microwaves. *American School and University* 43:47-49.

———. 1971. Vandals don't like the spotlight. *American School and University* 43:26-28.

American Teacher. 1977. AFT project to investigate school discipline, violence. *American Teacher* January: 4.

Anderson, B. 1973. School bureaucratization and alienation from high school. *Sociology of Education* 46:315-344.

Anderson, J. 1977. Vandalism in the Unified School District of Los Angeles County. Doctoral Dissertation, University of Southern California. Los Angeles.

Architectural Forum. 1971. Classrooms on a loop. *Architectural Forum* 135:47.

Armstrong, R. 1972. Student involvement. *Oregon: ERIC Clearinghouse on Educational Management,* no. 14.

Arnold, A. 1976. Vandalism in an inner city school administrative complex. Doctoral dissertation, University of California, Los Angeles.

Aronson, E., and Harris, T. 1975. Busing and racial tension: The jigsaw route to learning and liking. *Psychology Today* 8:43-50.

Asbury, H. 1928. *The Gangs of New York.* New York: Alfred E. Knopf.

Ashbaugh, C. 1969. High school student activism: Nine tested approaches for coping with conflict situations. *Nation's Schools* 83:94-96.

Babigian, G. 1971. How to defuse bomb threats with organization, planning. *Nation's Schools* 87:110, 112.

Bailey, S.K. 1970. *Disruption in urban public secondary schools.* Washington, D.C.: National Association of Secondary School Principals.

Baltimore City Public Schools. 1974. *Annual report of vandalism in selected great cities and Maryland counties,* 1973, 1974. Baltimore: Office of Research, Reports, and Records.

———. 1968. *Vandalism study of selected great cities, 1966-1967.* Baltimore: Division of Research and Development, Bureau of Records and Statistics.

Barker, R.G. and Gump, P. 1962. *Big school, small school: Studies of the effects of high school size upon the behavior and experiences of students.* Lawrence, Kans.: University of Kansas, Midwest Psychological Field Station.

Barnes, B. 18 June 1975. County school vandalism rising, senate panel told. *Washington Post.*

Bartlett, K. 1976. A self-reported study of participation in vandalism by the sophomore classes of three selected rural Ohio high schools. Doctoral dissertation, Ohio State University, Columbus, Oh.

Bates, W. 1962. Caste, class and vandalism. *Social Problems* 9:348–353.

Bates, W. and McJunkins, T. 1962. Vandalism and status differences. *Pacific Sociological Review* 2:89-92.

Baughman, P. 1971. *Vandalism and its prevention.* Los Angeles: California Association of School Business Officials.

Berger, M. 1974. *Violence in the schools: Causes and remedies.* Bloomington, Ind.: Phi Delta Kappa Educational Foundation.

Blauvelt, P. 1976. Understanding vandalism. Paper presented to National Association of School Security Directors, Bicentennial Conference, Dallas, Texas 11-16 July.

Bloch, A. 1977. The battered teacher. *Today's Education* 66:58-62.

Bower, E. 1954. Vandalism: An outgrowth of hostility, aggression and frustration. *Federal Probation* 18:12-14.

Bower, R. 1976. Vandalism in selected Florida schools. Doctoral dissertation, Florida Atlantic University, Boca Raton, Fla.

Bradley, C.E. 1967. Vandalism and protective devices: studies, conclusions, recommendations. *Proceedings of the Association of School Business Officials, United States and Canada,* 53:236-245.

Brady, E.D. 1972. Ten trends in school security. *Nation's Schools* 89:49.

Brenton, M. 1975. School vandalism. *Today's Education* 82:84-85.

Brickman, W. 1976. Vandalism and violence in school and society. *Intellect* 104:503.

Bried, R. 1969. Design your plant to avoid maintenance sore spots. *Nation's Schools* 83:100-102.

Briscoe, C. 1974. Project VITAL — juvenile offenders returning to school. *Clearinghouse* 48:411-415.

Brodsky, S.L. and Knudten, D.R. 1973. *Strategies for delinquency prevention in the schools.* Tuscaloosa, Ala.: University of Alabama.

Bromley, P. 1975. Student involvement through a communication system. *National Association of Secondary School Principals Bulletin,* 59:41-45.

Broski, D. 1977. Ohio school vandalism: Characteristics and preventive measures. Doctoral dissertation, University of Akron, Akron, Ohio.

Burton, L.W. 1975. Model school security system cuts crime. *Security World* June: 12-14.

Buss, W.G. 1971. *Legal aspects of crime investigation in the public schools.* Topeka, Kans.: National Organization on Legal Problems of Education.

Byerly, C.L. 1966. A school curriculum for prevention and remediation of deviancy. In *Social deviancy among youth,* ed. W.W. Wattenberg, pp. 221-257. National Society for the Study of Education, Yearbook no. 65, part I. Chicago: University of Chicago Press.

Caigan, R. 1971. Designing for use. *American School and University* 43:38-40.

California Association of School Business Officials. 1967. Deterring vandalism. California Association of School Business Officials Maintenance and Operations Research Committee, Southern Section, Fortieth Annual Conference.

California State Department of Education. 1973. *A report on conflict and violence in California's high schools.* Sacramento, Calif.

Cardinell, C.F. 1974. Let's get at the causes of youthful vandalism. *American School Board Journal* 161:68-69.

———. 1969. Relationship and interaction of selected personality characteristics of school principals and custodians with sociological variables to school vandalism. Doctoral dissertation, Michigan State University, East Lansing.

Carlton, S.A. 1974. Security notebook: surveying school security and costs. *Security World* 11:26-27, 46.

Casler, L. 1974. Are our public schools turning out warriors, not lovers? *American School Board Journal* 161:55-57.

Caudill, W. 1967. What works and what fails in school design. *Nation's Schools* 79:85-116.

Cavan, R. and Ferdinand, T. 1975. *Juvenile delinquency.* Philadelphia: J.B. Lippincott.

Center for Law and Education. 1975. Discipline and student rights. *Inequality in Education* 22:1-82.

Chasnoff, R.E. 1967. Structure of delinquency. *National Elementary Principal* 47:54.

Chesler, M. and Graham, P. n.d., *Alternative responses to school crises and experiments in police-school relations.* Ann Arbor, Mich.: The University of Michigan.

Children's Defense Fund. 1974. *Children out of school in America.* Cambridge, Mass.: Washington Research Project, Inc.

———. 1975. *Schools suspensions: Are they helping children?* Cambridge, Mass.: Washington Research Project, Inc.

Chilton, R. 1967. Middle class delinquency and specific offense analysis. In *Middle class juvenile delinquency*, ed. E. Vaz, New York: Harper and Row.

Christensen, R.H. 1975. Differences in administering discipline among minority schools, heterogeneous schools and predominantly all white secondary schools. Doctoral dissertation, Brigham Young University, Provo, Utah.

Clark, W. 1977. Violence in the public schools: A qualitative study of violence in the public schools. Doctoral dissertation, University of California, Berkeley.

Clement, S.L. 1975. School vandalism: Causes and cures. *National Association of Secondary School Principals Bulletin* 59:17-21.

Clements, C.B. 1976. The School Relations Bureau: A program of police intervention. In *Delinquency prevention and the schools: Emerging perspectives,* ed. E.A. Wenk, pp. 65-78. Beverly Hills, Calif.: Sage Publications.

Clinard, M.B. and Wade, A.L. 1958. Toward the delineation of vandalism as as sub-type in juvenile delinquency. *Journal of Criminal Law, Criminology and Police Science.* 48:493-499.

Cloward, R.A. and Ohlin, L.E. 1960. *Delinquency and opportunity.* New York: Free Press.

Cobb, M. 1953. Some suggestions for preventing discipline problems in the schools. *High Points* 35:12-13.

Cohen, S. 1973. Campaigning against vandalism. In *Vandalism*, ed. C. Ward. London: Architectural Press.

_____. 1971. Direction for research on adolescent school violence and vandalism. *British Journal of Criminology* 9:319-340.

_____. 1968. The politics of vandalism. *New Society* 12:872-878.

Colmey, J. and Valentine, T. 1961. Deterrents to vandalism. *American School Board Journal*, 142:11-13.

Colver, A. and Richter, J. 1971. "Yes" to a self-directed day. *Phi Delta Kappan* 53:111-112.

Coppock, N. 1973. School security. *Educational Management Review* 23:1-5.

Coursen, D. 1975. Vandalism prevention. *School Leadership Digest.* Arlington, Virginia: National Association of Elementary School Principals, Second Series 1.

Criminal Justice Newsletter. 1975. Educators split on school violence. *Criminal Justice Newsletter* 6:5.

Cross, J. 1976. Why so much violence in the schools? *American Vocational Journal.* 51:28-30.

Crowe, T.D.; Hanes, L.F.; Pesce, E.J.; and Riemer, A. 1976. *Crime prevention through environmental design: School demonstration plan.* Arlington, Virg.: Westinghouse Electric Corp.

Csikszentmihayli, M. and Larson, R. 1978. Intrinsic rewards in school crime. *Crime and Delinquency* 24:322-335.

Daniels, H. 1976. Vandalism: A comparative study of some of the effects of community education in public schools. Doctoral dissertation, Florida Atlantic University, Boca Raton.

Dauw, B. 1965. The high cost of vandalism. *Safety Education*, 44:3-7.

Debuzna, C. 1974. A study of school vandalism-causes and prevention measures currently found in selected secondary schools in cities throughout Alabama. Doctoral dissertation, University of Alabama, University.

DeCecco, J.P. and Richards, A.K. 1975. Civil war in the high schools. *Psychology Today* 9:51-56, 120.

_____. 1974. *Growing pains: Uses of school conflict.* New York: Aberdeen Press.

Delacoma, W. 1970. Vandalism—out of control? *Journal of Insurance Information* 31:15-17.

Demarest, M. 1973. School vandal: Scourge and symptom. *Learning* 1:35-37.

Denenberg, H.S. 1969. Insurance study, crime against small business. A report of the Small Business Administration transmitted to the Select Committee on Small Business, U.S. Senate, April 3, 1969.

Denver Area Welfare Council, Inc. 1954. *A Study of Vandalism.* Denver.

Deutsch, M. 1962. The 1960 swastika smearings: Analysis of the apprehended youth. *Merrill-Palmer Quarterly of Behavior and Development* 8:99-120.

Division of Alternative Programs. 1975. *Alternative programs in the Philadelphia public schools.* Philadelphia: School District of Philadelphia.

Ducey, M. 1976. *Vandalism in high schools: An exploratory discussion.* Chicago: Institute for Juvenile Research.

Dukiet, K. 1973. Spotlight on school security. *School Management* 17:16-18.

Dwyer, D. 1971. Police-school liaison programs is a positive prevention move. *National Police Journal* 13:21-23.

Educational Research Service. 1974. Losses due to vandalism, arson, and theft in public school systems, 1972-73. *ERS Research Memo.* Arlington, Virg.

_____. 1968. *Protecting Schools Against Vandalism.* Arlington, Virg.: Educational Research Service.

Education Policy Research Institute. 1978. Survey findings in 56 large urban districts: Press release. Washington, D.C.: Education Policy Research Institute of the Educational Testing Service.

Edwards, L. 1970. School property losses reach record heights. Insurance costs: up and almost away. *Nation's Schools* 85:51-55.

_____. 1971. How to reduce the cost of vandalism losses. Paper presented at National School Board Association, Philadelphia, Penn., April 1971.

Eliot, M. 1954. What is vandalism? *Federal Probation* 18:3-5.

Elliott, D.S. and Voss, H.L. 1974. *Delinquency and dropout.* Lexington, Mass.: Lexington Books, D.C. Heath and Company.

Ellison, W. 1974. An analysis of the impact of community schools on the reduction of vandalism in a selected district. Doctoral dissertation, University of Michigan, Ann Arbor.

Ellison, W.S. 1973. School vandalism: 100 million dollar challenge. *Community Education Journal* 3:27-33.

Emory, V. 1966. Vandalism and protective devices. *Proceedings of the Association of School Business Officials, United States and Canada* 52:233-237.

Emrich, R. 1978. The Safe School Study report: Evaluation and recommendations. *Crime and Delinquency* 24:266-276.

Ertukel, D. 1974. School security: A student point of view. *National Association of Secondary School Principals Bulletin* 58:44-49.

Etzioni, A. 1971. Violence. In *Contemporary Social Problems* ed. R. Merton and R. Nisbet New York: Harcourt Brace Jovanovich.

Fandt, E. 1961. A study of the practices of New Jersey boards of education in protecting school property against losses due to vandalism and malicious mischief. Doctoral dissertation, Rutgers University, New Brunswick, N.J.

Federal Bureau of Investigation. 1975. *Uniform Crime Reports: 1975.* Washington, D.C., U.S. Department of Justice.

Fielder, M. 1969. A diversified team approach to conflict intervention. *Educational Leadership* 27:15-18.

Foreman, E.G. 1967. Vandalism: Maintaining and protecting the school plant. *Catholic Schools,* September: 70-72.

Foster, H.L. 1971. To reduce violence: The interventionist teacher and aide. *Phi Delta Kappan* 53:59-62.

Franklin, A. 1961. The all-day neighborhood schools: Their role in delinquency prevention. *Crime and Delinquency*, 7:255-262.

Freese, W. 1971. Building and contents insurance. Paper presented at Iowa Association of School Business Officials, Council Bluffs, Iowa, April 1971.

Fresno City Unified School District. 1973. *Survey of burglary and vandalism occurrence and preventive measures in twenty-five large California school districts.* Summary Report. Fresno, Calif.: Office of Planning and Research Services.

Furno, O.F. and Wallace, L. 1972a. *Can you reduce your district's vandalism costs?* Baltimore, Md.: Baltimore City Public Schools, Division of Research and Development.

_____. 1972b. Vandalism: Recovery and prevention. *American School and University* 44:19-22.

Gallup, G.H. 1978. Ninth annual Gallup poll of public attitudes toward education. *Phi Delta Kappan* 59:33-45.

Gardner, J.C. 1972. Spotlighting school vandalism. *American School and University* 44:12.

Garrett, J.; Bass, S.; and Casserly, M. Studying school crime: A prescription for research-based prevention in *School Crime and Disruption* ed. E. Wenk and N. Harlow, Davis, California: Dialogue Books, 1978.

Gatti, D.J. 1976. Violence in the schools: When is it assault and when is it battery? *American Vocational Journal* 51:31-32.

Gazzolo, D. 1975. Portland named to test environmental crime study. *Journal of Housing* 32:434.

Gingery, S.L. 1946. Vandalism in schools. *School Business Affairs* September.

Glaser, D. 1973. *Routinizing evaluation: Getting feedback on effectiveness of crime and delinquency programs.* Rockville, Md.: National Institute of Mental Health.

Glueck, S. and Glueck, E. 1957. *Unraveling juvenile delinquency.* Cambridge, Mass.: Harvard University Press.

Gold, M. 1963. *Status-Forces in Delinquent Boys.* Ann Arbor, Mich.: Institute for Social Research.

Gold, M. and Reimer, D. 1975. Changing patterns of delinquent behavior among American 13 through 16 year olds: 1967-1972. *Crime and Delinquency Literature*, December.

Goldman, N. 1961. A socio-psychological study of school vandalism. *Crime and Delinquency* 7:221-230.

_____. 1969. School vandalism. *Education Digest* 26:1-4.

Goldmeier, H. 1974. Vandalism: The effects of unmanageable confrontations. *Adolescence* 9:49-56.

Goss v. Lopez (1975) 95 Ct. 729.

Gray, J. 1967. *The Teacher's Survival Guide*. Belmont, Calif.: Fearon Press.

Grealy, J.I. 1974a. Criminal activity in schools: What's being done about it? *National Association of Secondary School Principals Bulletin*, 38:73-78.

_____. 1974b. Safety and security in the school environment. *Security World* 11:42.

_____. 1975a. Hire experts as school security officers. *American School Board Journal* 162:34.

_____. 1975b. Making schools more secure. Paper presented at the Annual Convention of the American Association of School Administrators, Dallas, Texas, February 1975.

_____. 1975c. Nature and extent of school violence and vandalism. *School Security Journal* 2:25-29.

_____. 1975d. School violence: What can be done about it? *American School and University* 47:25-29.

_____. 1976. School security and systems planning. Paper presented at the 1976 International Security Conference, New York City, October 1976.

Greenberg, B. 1969. *School vandalism: A national dilemma. Final Report.* Menlo Park, Calif.: Stanford Research Institute.

_____. 1974. School vandalism: Its effects and paradoxical solutions. *Crime Prevention Review* 1:11-18.

Greenberg, B.; Friedlund, G.K.; Smyser, J.G.; and Fitzsimmons, S.C. 1975. *Program for the prevention and control of school vandalism and related burglaries.* Final Report. Menlo Park, Calif.: Stanford Research Institute.

Greenhalgh, J. 1973. Early warning systems assure safe schools. *School Management* 17:19-21, 36.

Greenstein, R. 1970. Can we lessen vandalism? *Instructor* 79:90-91.

Greider, C. 1970. Vandalism, symptomatic of our societal sickness. *Nation's Schools* 85:10.

Grimditch, R.E. 1973. How to cut down school vandalism. *Education Digest* 38:31-33.

Gudridge, B. 1969. *High school student unrest: How to anticipate protest, channel activism, and protect student rights.* Arlington, Virg.: National School Public Relations Association.

Haggart, S. 1971. *Program cost analysis in educational planning.* Santa Monica, Calif.: Rand Corporation.

Hamilton, J. 1976. Vandalism in Texas high schools: Nature, extent and prevention measures. Doctoral dissertation, Texas A&M University, College Station.

Haney, C. and Zimbardo, P. 1975. It's tough to tell a high school from a prison. *Psychology Today* 9:268.

Haney, S. 1973. School district reduces vandalism 65%. *American School and University* 46:29.

Harris, K.B. 1974. Reducing school violence and drug abuse. *Security World* 11:18-19, 44-45.

Hart, R.L. and Saylor, J.G., eds. 1970. *Student unrest: Threat or promise?* Washington, D.C.: Association for Supervision and Curriculum Development.

Hathaway, J.S., and Edwards, L.F., Jr. 1972. How to (just about) vandalproof every school in your district. *American School Board Journal* 159:27-31.

Havighurst, R. 1970. *A profile of the large city high school.* Washington, D.C.: National Association of Secondary School Principals.

Herbers, J. 9 May 1969. High school unrest rises, alarming U.S. educators. *The New York Times* 30:1, 30.

Herrick, M. 1961. Discipline in the schools. *Crime and Delinquency* 7:213-220.

Hevern, H. 1977. An analysis of the extent, costs and prevention of vandalism in Hawaii public secondary schools. Doctoral dissertation, University of Southern California. Los Angeles.

Hindelang, M. and McDermott, M. 1977. *Criminal victimization in urban schools.* Albany, N.Y.: Criminal Justice Research Center.

Hirschi, T. 1969. *Causes of delinquency*, Berkeley, Calif.: University of California Press.

Holman, B. 1975. National trends and student unrest. *Security World* 12:43-44.

Howard, J.L. 1978. Factors in School Vandalism. *Journal of Research and Development in Education* 2:53-62.

Hubbard, S. 1973. Getting the most wear from school entrances. *American School and University* 45:67-68.

Hudgins, A.C., Jr. 1975. *School administrators and the courts: A review of recent decisions.* Arlington, Virg.: Educational Research Service.

Hunt, J. 1969. Principals report on student protest. *American Education* 5:4-5.

Ingraham v. *Wright* (438 U.S. 651).

Institute for Development of Educational Activities. 1969. *Dissent and disruption in the schools: A handbook for school administrators.* Dayton, Ohio.

——. 1974. *Problem of school security.* Dayton, Ohio.

Irwin, F. 1975. A Study of features for lessening vandalism for consideration in the planning of education facilities. Doctoral dissertation, University of Tennessee, Knoxville.

Jackson, M. 1976. *Schools that change: A report on success strategies for disruption, violence, and vandalism in public high schools.* Washington, D.C.: National Institute of Education (ED 151-965).

Jacob, S. 1967. Let's do something about vandalism. *American County Government* October.

James, H. 1974. How secure is your classroom? *Teacher* 91:42-43.

Jeffery, C. 1971. *Crime prevention through environmental design.* Beverly Hills, Calif.: Sage Publications.

Jones, J.W. 1973. *Discipline crisis in schools: The problem, causes and search for solutions.* Arlington, Virg.: Education USA Special Report, National School Public Relations Association.

Juillerat, E.E. 1966. Burn the school—that'll show 'em! *Fire Journal* 60:16-20.

_____. 1972. Fire and vandals: How to make them both unwelcome in your school. *American School Board Journal* 159:23-26.

_____. 1974. For worried school districts: Here's lots of sensible advice for lasting ways to cut down school vandalism. *American School Board Journal* 161:64-69.

Juvenile Justice Digest. 1975. School violence hearings indicate chaos in American public education. *Juvenile Justice Digest* 3:8-10.

Kaser, T. 21 May 1975. Burglary, vandalism rate soars in island schools. *Honolulu Advertiser.*

Katzenmayer, W. and Surrat, J. 1975. Police at the schoolhouse. *Phi Delta Kappan* 57:206-207.

Kelly, D.H. 1976. Track position, school misconduct, and youth deviance: A test of the interpretive effect of school commitment. *Urban Education* 10:379-388.

Kelly, R.L. 1973. Vandalism, safety and security. *School Business Affairs* 39:164-166.

Kemble, E. 1975. Violence in the schools and public school policies. Paper presented at the Annual Meeting of the Council for Education Research and Development, Washington, D.C., December 1975.

Kepler, R. n.d. Management in curbing vandalism costs. Hagerstown, Md.: Board of Education of Washington County.

Kett, J.F. 1977. *Rites of Passage: Adolescence in America.* New York: Basic Books.

Keve, P.W. and Young, K.R. 1961. School and court working together. *Crime and Delinquency* 7:242-248.

Kiernan, O.B. 1975. *School violence and vandalism.* Reston, Virg.: National Association of Secondary School Principals.

Kihss, P. 3 December 1968. Youths clash with police and teachers are beaten. *The New York Times.*

Klaus, D., with Gunn, A. 1977. *Serious school crime: A review of the literature.* Washington, D.C.: American Institutes for Research.

Knowles, C.D. 1973. *Alternative programs: A grapevine survey.* Davis, Calif.: National Council on Crime and Delinquency.

Knudten, R.D. 1976. Delinquency programs in schools: A survey. In *Delinquency prevention and the schools: Emerging perspectives*, ed. E.A. Wenk, pp. 53-64. Beverly Hills, Calif.: Sage Publications.

Kobetz, R.W. 1973. Juvenile vandalism: The billion dollar prank. *Police Chief* 40:32-34.

Koch, E.L. 1975. School vandalism and strategies of social control. *Urban Education* 10:54-72.

Kolstad, C.K. 1974. Microwaves stop school vandals. *Security World* 11:20-21, 54.

Kravontka, S.J. 1974. CCTV system design for school security. *Security World* 11:22-23, 48-49.

Kressel, L. 28 March 1971. Dogs in vandalism. *The New York Times.*

Kvaraceus, W.C. 1954. *Juvenile delinquency and the schools.* Yonkers, N.Y.: World Book Co.

Lakewood City (Ohio) Board of Education. 1971. *Dealing with aggressive behavior: A curriculum for middle school and junior high.* 2 vols.: Teacher's manual, student book. Cleveland, Ohio: Educational Research Council of America.

Lalli, M. and Savitz, L. 1976. The fear of crime in the school enterprise and its consequences. *Education and Urban Society* 8:401-416.

Laub, E.B. 1961. The story of "You and the Law." *Crime and Delinquency* 7:237-241.

Law Enforcement Assistance Administration. 1975. Cost of school crime exceeds half billion dollars each year. *LEAA Newsletter* 4:26.

———. 1975. Super security program in city schools cuts after-hours crime. *LEAA Newsletter* 4:27.

Leftwich, D. 1977. A study of vandalism in selected public schools in Alabama. Doctoral dissertation, University of Alabama, University.

Lerner, S.E. and Linder, R.L. 1974. Drugs in the elementary school. *Journal of Drug Education* 4:317-322.

Lesser, P. 1976. Violence in urban schools: An organizational approach. Paper presented to the Second National Conference on Urban Education, Milwaukee, Wisconsin, November 1976.

———. 1978. Poverty, school control patterns, and student disruption. Riverside, Calif.: National Council on Crime and Delinquency.

Levine, A.; Cary, E.; and Divoky, D. 1973. *The rights of students: The basic ACLU guide to a student's rights.* New York: Discus Books.

Levine, S. 1972. Speaking out. *National Elementary Principal* 52:67.

L'Hote, J.D. 1970. Detroit fights theft and arson. *American School and University* 42:19-21.

Licht, K. 1972. School security and safety. Speech given before Association of School Business Officials Annual Meeting, Chicago, Illinois, October 1972.

Lippman, H. 1954. Vandalism as an outlet for aggression. *Federal Probation* 18:5-6.

Lucas, W.L. 1977. Experiences in a large city school system. In *Violence in schools*, ed. J.M. McPartland and E.L. McDill, pp. 71-76. Lexington, Ma.: Lexington Books, D.C. Heath and Company.

Macaluso, J. 1976. A Study to determine the factors relating to the cost of vandalism in a large southern urban public school system. Doctoral dissertation, University of Southern Mississippi, Jacksonville.

McCord, Jr. 1973. Vandalism: A special report. *Nation's Schools* 92:31-37.

McDill, E. and Rigsby, L. 1973. *Structure and process in secondary schools.* Baltimore: Johns Hopkins University Press.

McGovern, E. and Piers, M.W. 1972. Child care for non-violence. *Childhood Education* 49:9-13.

McGowan, W. 1973. Crime control in public schools: Space age solutions. *National Association of Secondary School Principals Bulletin* 57:43-48.

McGuire, W. 1975. What can we do about violence? *Today's Education* 64:22-23.

———. 1976. Violence in the schools. *NEA Reporter* 15:3.

McKenna, J. 1974. Crime in the schools. *New York Affairs*, 1:3-13.

McPartland, J.P. and McDill, E.L. 1975. *Research on crime in the schools*. Baltimore: Center for Social Organization of Schools, Johns Hopkins University.

———. 1977. *Violence in the schools*. Lexington, Mass.: Lexington Books, D.C. Heath and Company.

Madison, A. 1970. *Vandalism: The not-so-senseless crime*. New York: Seabury Press.

Manella, F.L. 1970. A program to cope with youth violence in schools. *Law and Order* 18:24-27.

Mannheim, H. 1954. The problem of vandalism in Great Britain. *Federal Probation* 18:14-15.

Mapes, G. 10 December 1968. Costly mischief: Vandalism by youths takes a mounting toll at schools and firms. *Wall Street Journal.*

Marburger, C.L. 1966. School-community relations and maladjusted youth. In *Social deviancy among youth*, ed. W.W. Wattenberg pp. 258-279. National Society for the Study of Education, Yearbook no. 65, part 1. Chicago: University of Chicago Press.

Marcase, M.P. 1976. *Discipline in the Philadelphia public schools: A working document*. Philadelphia: Board of Education of Philadelphia.

Martin, J.M. 1961. *Juvenile vandalism: A study of its nature and prevention*. Springfield, Ill.: Charles C. Thomas.

Marvin, M. 1976. *Planning assistance programs to reduce school violence and disruption*. Philadelphia: Research for Better Schools.

Maslow, A. 1942. A comparative approach to the problem of destructiveness. *Psychiatry* 5:517-522.

Mays, J. 1963. Vandalism and violence. *Crime and Social Structure*. New York: Humanities Press.

Metzner, S. 1968. School violence in historical perspective. Paper presented to the American Educational Research Association in Los Angeles, February 1968.

Michelson, B.E. 1956. Vandalism in our schools. *Education Digest* September 13-15.

Middleton, L. 25 February 1977. Crime rising in schools, report says. *The Washington Star.*

Miller, L.E. and Beer, D. 1974. Security system pays off. *American School and University* 46:39-40.

Miller, W.B. *Violence by youth gangs and youth groups in major American cities*. Cambridge, Mass.: Harvard Law School, Center for Criminal Justice.

Modern Schools. 1972. Floodlighting is multipurpose. *Modern Schools*, April.

———. 1971. Lightup for nighttime protection. *Modern Schools*, March.

———. 1973. Protect your school buildings with electric security systems. *Modern Schools*, April:6-8.

———. 1974. Ultrasonic sound protects New Jersey School. *Modern Schools* March:12-13.

———. 1974. Vandalism, fire, theft: What can you do? *Modern Schools* March:8-10.

Moffitt, F. 1964. Vandals' rocks can't reach flying schoolhouse. *Nation's Schools* 74:22.

Moreo, D. 1969. Seattle schools and the 40/60/40 syndrome. *Urban Review* 4:5-8.

Morgan, J.B. 1952. *The psychology of the unadjusted school child*. New York: The MacMillan Company.

Moulden, W.E. 1974. Schools and delinquency: Four teacher corps approaches. *Juvenile Justice* 25:47-55.

Mullins, J. 1974. Yerba Buena crisis counseling project: The interagency team approach. San Jose, Calif.

Munnelly, R.J. 1971. Is it time to break the silence on violence? *Elementary School Journal* 71:237-243.

Murillo, R. 1977. Vandalism and school attitudes. Doctoral dissertation, Florida State University, Tallahasee.

Murphy, H.H. 1973. Vandals, arsonists, bombs, dogs. Paper presented at American Association of School Administrators Annual Convention, San Francisco, March 1973.

Murphy, J. 1954. The answer to vandalism may be found in the home. *Federal Probation* 18:8-10.

Murray, C. 1976. *The link between learning disabilities and juvenile delinquency*. Washington, D.C.: American Institutes for Research.

National Association of School Security Directors. 1975. *Uniform report of school losses and offenses*. Miami.

National Association of Secondary School Principals. 1976. Controlling disruptive behavior. *The Practitioner* 2:5.

————. 1977. *Disruptive Youth: Causes and Solutions*. Reston, Virg.

National Center for Education Statistics. 1976. *Survey of offenses and property losses—disclaimers and data limitations*. Washington, D.C.: U.S. Department of Health, Education, and Welfare, Office of Education.

National Clearinghouse for Criminal Justice Planning and Architecture. 1975. *Policy development seminar on architecture, design and criminal justice*. Proceedings of an LEAA Conference on Architectural Design and the Problems of Security. Rochester, Michigan, June 1975.

National Commission on the Reform of Secondary Education. 1973. *The reform of secondary education: A report to the public and the profession*. New York: McGraw-Hill.

National Committee for Citizens in Education. 1975. *Violence in our schools: What to know about it and what to do about it*. Columbia, Md.

National Education Association. 1975. *Danger—school ahead: Violence in the public schools*. Washington, D.C.

————. 1975. Educational neglect: Research papers for conference on educational neglect. Washington, D.C.

————. 1971. *Reference on vandalism and security systems in public schools*. Washington, D.C.

_____.1956. Teacher opinion on pupil behavior, 1955-1956. *Research Bulletin of the National Education Association* 34:51-107.

_____. 1976. Violence in the schools: Violence permeates our schools; Who's to blame for school violence?; One teacher's struggle against school violence; What associations are doing about school violence. *NEA Reporter* 15:3-9.

_____.1973. Teacher opinion poll. *Today's Education* 62:7.

_____. 1974. Teacher opinion poll. *Today's Education* 63:105.

National Fire Protection Association. 1973. *A study of school fires.* Boston, Mass.

_____. 1966. Fires and fire losses classified, 1965. *Fire Journal* 60:33-38.

National School Public Relations Association. 1975. *Discipline crisis in schools: The problem, causes and search for solutions.* Arlington, Virg.

_____. 1970. Urban school crisis: The problem and solutions proposed by the HEW Task Force on Urban Education. Washington, D.C.

National School Resource Network. 1980. *School Violence Prevention Manual.* Cambridge, Mass.: Oelgeschlager, Gunn and Hain, Inc.

National Urban League, Inc. 1971. *The problem of discipline/control and security in our schools.* Position Paper no. 1. New York.

Nation's Schools. 1965. Can your district use some of these ideas for curbing vandalism? *Nation's Schools* 76:30-32.

_____. 1972. Curbing vandalism costs. *Nation's Schools* 89:46-49.

_____. 1974. Review board gives students a day in court. *Nation's Schools* 93:46.

_____. 1964. Rich schools, poor schools face the same problem: Vandalism. *Nation's Schools* 74:29.

_____. 1972. Upgraded glazings present a stronger image: Plant operation. *Nation's Schools* 89:90, 94.

_____. 1968. Vandalism: A dirty word for 8 of 10 schoolmen. School administrator opinion poll. *Nation's Schools* 81:66-67.

_____. 1973. Vandalism: Take Tempting Targets Out. *Nation's Schools* 92:44.

_____. 1968. Vandalism: How schools combat vandalism. *Nation's Schools* 81:58-67.

_____. 1960. Vandalism: School administrators' opinion poll findings. *Nation's Schools* 66:55, 92.

_____. 1975. Cops in, robbers out. *Nation's Schools and Colleges* 2:12.

Nedurian, V. 1972. Guidelines—Cooperation between school officials and police departments. *Nolpe School Law Journal* 2:57-65.

Neill, S.B. 1971. *Vandalism and violence: Innovative strategies reduce cost to schools.* Arlington, Virg.: National School Public Relations Association.

_____. 1976. Causes of school violence and vandalism. *Education Digest* 41:6-9.

_____. 1975. *Violence and Vandalism: Current Trends in School Policies and Programs.* Arlington, Virg.: National School Public Relations Association.

Nelken, I. and Kline, S. 1971. *Destruction or loss of school property: Analysis and suggestions for improvement of school security.* Chico, Calif.: California State University, Educational System Planning.

Nemy, E. 14 June 1975. Violence in schools now seen as norm across the nation. *The New York Times.*

Neville, H.C. 1974. School arson: Is your protection adequate? *American School and University* 47:31-32.

New Jersey School Boards Association, Ad hoc Committee to Study Vandalism. 1975. *School vandalism survey.* Trenton, N.J.

Newman, O. 1972. *Design directives for achieving defensible space.* Washington, D.C.: National Institute of Law Enforcement and Criminal Justice.

Nielsen, M. 1971. Vandalism in schools: A 200 million dollar problem. *Oregon School Study Council Bulletin* 15.

Nolte, C. 1975. Why you need a student grievance plan and how you can have a reasonable one. *American School Board Journal* 162:38-40.

Nowakowski, R. 1966. Vandals and vandalism in the schools: An analysis of vandalism in large school systems and a description of ninety-three vandals in Dade County schools. Doctoral dissertation. University of Miami.

O'Grince, S. and Hodgins, H.S. 1968. Public school vandalism. *American School and University* 40:30-32.

Olson, C. 1970. Developing school pride, reducing vandalism: A guide for student leaders. San Diego, Calif.: San Diego City Schools.

Olson, C., and Carpenter, J.B. 1971. *A survey of techniques used to reduce vandalism and delinquency in schools.* McLean, Virg.: Research Analysis Corp.

Ornstein, A.C. and Freeman, J. 1971. On high school violence. *Journal of Secondary Education* 46:9-15.

Pablant, P. and Baxter, J. 1975. Environmental correlates of school vandalism. *Journal of the American Institute of Planners* 41:270-279.

Page, C. 1977. Vandalism: It happens every night. *Nation's Cities* 15:6-7.

Palmer, J. 1975. A study of the community education program as a deterrent of violence and vandalism in a small rural michigan community. Doctoral dissertation, University of Michigan, Ann Arbor.

Panel on School Safety. 1972. A safer environment for learning. New York: Academy for Educational Development.

Parkway School District. 1974. *Vandalism: Environmental ecological education project.* Chesterfield, Mo.

Piersma, P. 1972. *The legal rights of secondary school children charged with an act of delinquency or violation of school laws: Handbook for school personnel 1972.* Ann Arbor, Mich.: University of Michigan, ERIC Counseling and Personnel Services Center.

Platzker, J. 1966. How much do we know about windowless schools? *Better Light Better Sight News* July-August.

Polk, K. 1976. Schools and the delinquency experience. In *Delinquency prevention and the schools: Emerging perspectives*, ed. E.A. Wenk, pp. 21-44. Beverly Hills, Calif.: Sage Publications.

Polk, K. and Schafer, W. 1972. *Schools and delinquency.* Englewood Cliffs, N.J.: Prentice-Hall.

Powell, J.W. 1972. School security: An emerging professionalism. *American School and University* 44:12-15.

Powell, W.C. 1976. Education intervention as a preventive measure. In *Delinquency prevention and the schools: Emerging perspectives*, ed. E.A. Wenk, pp. 105-115. Beverly Hills, Calif.: Sage Publications.

President's Commission on Law Enforcement and Administration of Justice, Task Force on Juvenile Delinquency. 1967. *Task force report: Juvenile delinquency and youth crime.* Washington, D.C.: U.S. Government Printing Office.

Prewer, R.R. 1958. Some observations on window-smashing. *British Journal of Delinquency* 9:104-113.

Pringle, M.K. 1974. The roots of violence and vandalism. *Community Health* 6:84-91.

Pritchard, R., and Wedra, V. 1975. *A resource manual for reducing conflict and violence in California schools.* Sacramento, Calif.: California School Boards Association.

Probst, T. 1961. How to cut down vandalism. *Nation's Schools* 68:64-68.

Project for the Fair Administration of Student Discipline. 1975. *Student rights and school discipline: Bibliography.* Ann Arbor: University of Michigan.

Pucinski, R. 1970. Results of survey on student unrest in the nation's high schools. *Congressional Record*: February 23, 1970:E1178-E1180.

Rawlins, R. 1964. Solutions to million dollar glass problems. *American School Board Journal* 149:40-41.

Reagen, M.V. 1973. Suspension and expulsion and problems of school security. Paper presented at the National Institute of the National Conference of Christians and Jews, Miami Beach, October-November 1973.

Rector, J.M. 1975. School violence and vandalism: A congressional perspective. *Security World* 12:41-43.

Redmond, J.F. 1968. *Personnel security officer's manual.* Chicago, Ill.: Board of Education.

Reeves, D.E. 1972. Protecting against fire and vandalism. *American School and University* 44:62-66.

Reiss, M.H. 1974. Selecting instrusion devices for your school. *Security World* 11:24-25, 57.

Reslock, L. 1971. *Manual on property protection.* Los Angeles: Los Angeles Unified School Department, Administrative Services Branch.

Reutter, E.E., Jr. 1975. *The courts and student conduct.* Topeka, Kans.: National Organization on Legal Problems of Education.

Rich, C. 1975. Violence erupts in the classroom: Area schools face trend to violence. *Evening Bulletin* (Philadelphia), 29 September 1975.

Richards, P. 1976. Patterns of middle class vandalism: A case study of suburban adolescence. Doctoral dissertation, Northwestern University, Evanston, Illinois.

Rideout, S. 1976. *Buying time: A story of student involvement.* Pittsburgh: Pittsburgh Board of Education.

Rigdon, V.D. 1976. School's security man tries to be a friend, too. *Montgomery County Sentinel*, 16 December 1976.

Ritterband, P. 1976. Ethnicity and school disorder. *Education and Urban Society* 8:383-400.

Ritterband, P. and Silberstein, R. 1973. Group disorders in the public schools. *American Sociological Review* 38:461-467.

Robert F. Kennedy Memorial. 1974. *Student pushout: Victim of a continued resistance to desegregation*. Washington, D.C.: Southern Regional Council.

_____. 1975. *Suspensions and due process: An analysis of recent Supreme Court decisions on student rights*. Washington, D.C.

Rose, F. 1977. Effect of violence and vandalism on the completion of the educational process. Doctoral dissertation, University of Iowa, Iowa City.

Ross, D.M. 1974. 1973 state education legislation and activity: Schools, students and services, a survey of the states. Denver, Colorado: Education Commission of the States.

Rowe, W.; Murphy, H.; and DeCsipkes, R. 1974. A behavior program for problem students. *Personnel and Guidance Journal* 52:609-612.

Roye, W.J. 1971. Law and order in classroom and corridor. National Center for Research and Information on Equal Education Opportunity. Tipsheet no. 6.

Rubel, R. 1977a. Assumptions underlying programs used to prevent or reduce student violence in secondary schools. Washington, D.C.: Law Enforcement Assistance Administration.

_____. 1977b. Data on student crimes in schools: What to collect, where to find them, and problems to avoid. Washington, D.C.: Law Enforcement Assistance Administration.

_____. 1977c. *The Unruly School: disorders, disruption, and crimes*. Lexington, Mass.: Lexington Books, D.C. Heath and Company.

_____. 1978. Analysis and critique of HEW's Safe School Study to the Congress. *Crime and Delinquency* 24:257-265.

Safe School Study. 1977. Washington, D.C.: National Institutes of Education.

San Diego Schools. 1968. A Summary of Security Force Survey Based on Eighteen Reporting Urban School Districts. San Diego: San Diego Schools, Department of Administration and Research.

Sanders, S.G. and Yarborough, J. 1976. Bringing order to an inner-city middle school. *Phi Delta Kappan* 58:333-334.

Schafer, W.E., and Polk, K. 1967. Delinquency in the schools. In *Task force report: Juvenile delinquency and youth crime*. The President's Commission on Law Enforcement and the Administration of Justice, Task Force on Juvenile Delinquency. Washington, D.C.: U.S. Government Printing Office.

Schnabolk, C. 1974. Safeguarding the school against vandalism; special report: Planning the learning environment. *Nation's Schools* 94:29-36.

Schofield, D. 1975. Student rights and student discipline. *School Leadership Digest No. 13*. Arlington, Virg.: National Association of Elementary School Principals.

School Management. 1965. How one district licked vandalism *School Management* 9:93-94.

———. 1973. Keep it looking like new. *School Management* 17:22-23.

———. 1967. Preventing school vandalism: Connect your school with police headquarters. *School Management* 11:19.

———. 1967. Putting an end to vandalism. *School Management* 11:18.

———. 1966. Vandalism: How one district fights it and wins. *School Management* 10:101-105.

School Progress. 1970. Maintenance operations. *School Progress* 39:40-44.

———. 1971. Vandalism. *School Progress* 40:50-51.

School Stability Resource Team. 1971. Stability and disruption in the public schools of New York City, New York. New York: New York Board of Education.

Schuchter, A. 1976. Schools and delinquency prevention strategies. In *Delinquency prevention and the schools: Emerging perspectives*, ed. E.A. Wenk, pp. 45-51. Beverly Hills, Calif.: Sage Publications.

Schwartz, S. 1973. A new way to fight school vandalism. *American School and University* 45:54-55.

Scott, C. 1954. Vandalism and our present day pattern of living. *Federal Probation* 18:10-12.

Scott, J. and El-Assal, Mohamed. 1969. Multiversity, university size, university quality, and student protest: An empirical study. *American Sociological Review* 34:702-709.

Security Systems Digest. 1975. Violence, vandalism threatens destruction of American schools. *Security Systems Digest* 6:1-4.

Security World. 1974. School security issue. *Security World* 11.

Seits, L.D. 1976. *Fear, tension, violence: The ugly part of school.* Evansville, Ind.: Evansville Press.

Sentelle, S. 1971. The keeping of the keys. *American School and University* 44:40-41.

Severino, M. 1972. Who pays, or who should pay, when young vandals smash things up in your schools? *American School Board Journal* 159:33-34.

Shalloo, J. 1954. Vandalism: Whose responsibility? *Federal Probation* 18:6-8.

Sharp, J.S. 1964. Proper design limits vandalism. *American School Board Journal* 149:22-23.

Shaw, W. 1973. Vandalism is not senseless. *Law and Order* 12:15-19.

Slater, J. 1974. Death of a high school. *Phi Delta Kappan* 56:251-254.

Slaybaugh, D. 1973. School security survey. *School Product News* June.

———. 1974. School security survey. *School Product News* June.

———. 1975. School security survey. *School Product News* June:10-15.

Slaybaugh, D. and Koneval, V.L. 1970. The high cost of vandalism. *School Product News*.

Smith, D.C. 1966. Vandalism in selected Southern California school districts: Nature, extent, and preventive measures. Doctoral dissertation, University of Southern California, Los Angeles.

Smith, D.H., ed. 1973. *Disruptive students*. Albany, N.Y.: New York State Education Department, Bureau of School Social Services.

Smith, P.M. 1952. The schools and juvenile delinquency. *Sociology and Social Research* 37:85-91.

Smith, V.; Barr, R.; and Burke, D. 1974. *Optional alternative public schools*. Bloomington, Ind.: Phi Delta Kappan Educational Foundation.

Spady, W. 1974. Authority system of the school and student unrest: A theoretical exploration. In *Uses of the Sociology of Education* National Society for the Study of Education, 73rd Yearbook. Chicago: University of Chicago Press.

Spalding, T. 1971. Door hardware to check vandalism. *School Management* 15:30-31.

Stanford Research Institute. 1975. *Program for the prevention and control of vandalism and related burglaries*. Final report, Menlo Park, Calif.

Stein, H. and Martin, J. 1962. Swastika offender: Variations in etiology, behavior and psycho-social characteristics. *Social Problems* 10:56-70.

Steinmetz, R.C. 1966. Current arson problems. Part 1. *Fire Journal* 60:23-25, 31.

_____. 1966. Current arson problems. Part 2. *Fire Journal* 60:33-37.

Stinchcombe, A. 1964. *Rebellion in a high school*. Chicago: Quadrangle Books.

Stretton, E. 1977. A study of school vandalism in junior high schools and middle schools in the state of Indiana. Doctoral dissertation, Indiana University, Bloomington.

Strom, M. 1974. School fires: Part of our overall crime problem. *Security World*, March: 20-23.

Strumpf, M. 1972. Maximum security at minimum cost. *School Management* 16:28-29.

Stullken, E.H. 1953. The schools and the delinquency problem. *Journal of Criminal Law, Criminology, and Police Science* 43:563-577.

Sullivan, R. 1972. School disruption: A survey of the literature. New York: Academy of Education Development.

Talmadge, K. and Horst, D. 1975. *A practical guide to measuring project impact on student achievement*. Los Altos, Calif.: RMC Research Corp.

Thistle, F. 1974. It's time we discussed the violence in America's schools. *PTA Magazine* 69:15-17.

Tien, J.M. and Reppetto, T.A. 1975. Elements of crime prevention through environmental design (CPTED): Annotated bibliography. Arlington, Virg.: Westinghouse Electric Corp.

_____. 1975. Crime/environment targets. Arlington, Virg.: Westinghouse Electric Corp.

Tien, M.J., Reppetto, T.A., and Hanes, L.F. 1975. *Elements of CPTED*. Arlington, Virg.: Westinghouse Electric Corp.

Time. 1975. The crime wave. *Time* 105:10-24.

_____. 1967. Schools and the summer. *Time* 90:17.

Tinto, V. undated. Antisocial patterning of deviant behavior in school. Syracuse University, Syracuse, N.Y.

Tobias, J. and LaBlanc, T. 1977. Malicious destruction of property in the suburbs. *Adolescence* 12:111-114.

Today's Education. 1972. Assaults on teachers. *Today's Education* 61:30-32, 69-71.

Tonigan, R. 1970. New ways to trip up vandals. *School Management* 14:20.

Totin, J., Jr. 1966. School vandalism: An overview. *Proceedings of the Association of School Business Officials, United States and Canada* 52:237-239.

Underwood, E.W. 1968. Opinions differ: Ways of fighting vandalism. *Today's Education* 57:29-32.

United Federation of Teachers. 1974. *Security in the schools: Tips for guarding the safety of teachers and students.* New York.

U.S. Children's Bureau. 1968. *Nation's Youth.* Washington, D.C.: Department of Health, Education and Welfare, Children's Bureau Publication no. 460.

U.S. Congress, House, Committee on Education and Labor, Subcommittee on Education. 1973. *Safe Schools Act: Hearing on H.R. 2650,* 93rd Cong., 1st sess., 26 February 1973.

U.S. Congress, 1974. The Education Amendments of 1974, sec. 825, Safe School Study Act. 93rd Cong., 21 August 1974.

U.S. Congress, House, Committee on Education and Labor, Subcommittee on Equal Opportunities. 1976. *Oversight hearing on the Juvenile Justice and Delinquency Prevention Act,* 94th Cong., 2nd sess., 29 June 1976.

U.S. Congress, Senate, Committee on the Judiciary, Subcommittee to Investigate Juvenile Delinquency. 1975a. *Our nation's schools—a report card: "A" in school violence and vandalism.* Washington, D.C.: U.S. Government Printing Office.

U.S. Congress, Senate, Committee on the Judiciary, Subcommittee to Investigate Juvenile Delinquency. 1975b. *Hearings on school violence and vandalism: The nature, extent, and cost of violence and vandalism in our nation's schools.* 94th Cong., 1st sess., 16-17 April 1975.

U.S. Congress, Senate, Committee on the Judiciary, Subcommittee to Investigate Juvenile Delinquency. 1975c. *Hearings on school violence and vandalism: Models and strategies for change.* 94th Cong., 1st sess., 17 September 1975.

U.S. Congress, Senate, Committee on the Judiciary, Subcommittee to Investigate Juvenile Delinquency. 1977. *Challenge for the third century: Education in a safe environment—final report on the nature and prevention of school violence and vandalism.* Washington, D.C.: U.S. Government Printing Office.

U.S. News & World Report. 1968. Violence hits schools, colleges. *U.S. News & World Report* May 20:36-38.

――――. 1969. U.S. teachers―targets of violence. *U.S. News & World Report* November 17:80.

――――. 1973. More muscle in the fight to stop violence in schools. *U.S. News & World Report* April 16:113-116.

――――. 1974. Vandalism―a billion dollars a year and getting worse. *U.S. News & World Report* June 24:37-40.

――――. 1975. Violence in schools: Now a crackdown. *U.S. News & World Report* April 14:37-40.

――――. 1976. Terror in schools. *U.S. News & World Report* January 26:52-55.

University of Oregon, ERIC Clearinghouse on Educational Management. 1976. *Vandalism prevention: The best of ERIC*, no. 20. Eugene, Ore.

Van Avery, D. 1975. Contrasting solutions for school violence: II. The humanitarian approach. *Phi Delta Kappan* 57:177-178.

Van Patten, J.J. 1976. Violence and vandalism in our schools. *Journal of Thought* 7:180-190.

Vestermark, S.D., Jr. 1971. *Responses to collective violence in threat or act.* McLean, Virginia: Human Sciences Research, Inc.

Vestermark S. and Blauvelt P. 1978. *Controlling crime in the school: A complete security handbook for administrators.* West Nyack, N.Y.: Parker Publishing Company.

Vicino, F.L. and Peterson, D. 1974. *Mesa, Arizona, Public Schools: Vandalism and theft analysis, 1973-74.* Mesa, Ariz.: Mesa Public Schools.

Virginia Division of Justice and Crime Prevention. 1974. School security shows success in Alexandria. *DJCP Progress* 2:2-3.

Wade, A. 1967. Social processes in the act of juvenile vandalism. In *Criminal Behavior Systems*, ed. M. Clinard and R. Quinney. New York: Holt, Rinehardt and Winston.

Ward, C., ed. 1973. *Vandalism.* London: Architectural Press.

Watson, B. 1976. Schooling, violence and vandalism: Promising politics and policy alternatives. Report for the House Committee on Education and Labor Subcommittee on Equal Opportunity, in oversight hearings on the Juvenile Justice and Delinquency Prevention Act, 29 June 1976.

Watson, B. and Darling-Hammond, L. 1978. Violence and vandalism in schools: Evidence for policy alternatives. *Cross Reference* 1:60-69.

Wattenberg, W.W., ed. 1966. *Social deviancy among youth.* National Society for the Study of Education, Yearbook no. 65, part 1. Chicago: University of Chicago Press.

Weeks, S. 1976. Security against vandalism: It takes facts, feelings, and facilities. *American School and University* 48:37-46.

Wegener, P.C. 1977. CPTED in Schools. *Nation's Cities* 15:22-25.

Weinmayr, V.M. 1969. Vandalism by design: A critique. *Landscape Architecture* 59:286.

Weintraub, R., and Morley, S. 1974. *Youth and the administration of justice: A model educational program on law and citizenship for schools.* Pasadena, Calif.: Constitutional Rights Foundation.

Weiss, N. 1974. Vandalism. An environmental concern. *National Association of Secondary School Principals Bulletin* 58:6-9.

Wells, E. 1971. *Vandalism and violence: Innovative strategies reduce in schools.* Education U.S.A. Special Report. Arlington, Virginia: National School Public Relations Association.

Wenk, E.A. 1975. Juvenile justice and the public schools: Mutual benefit through education reform. *Juvenile Justice* 26:7-14.

Wenk, E.A., ed. 1976. *Delinquency prevention and the schools: Emerging perspectives.* Beverly Hills, Calif.: Sage Publications.

Wenk. E.A. 1976. Schools and the community: A model for participatory problem-solving. In *Delinquency prevention and the schools: Emerging perspectives,* ed. E.A. Wenk. pp. 9-20. Beverly Hills, Calif.: Sage Publications.

Wenk, E., and Harlow, N., eds. 1978. *School Crime and Disruption.* Davis, Calif.: Dialogue Books.

Whitaker, J.D. 1976. $100,000 damage laid to 6 children. *Washington Post.* 21 December 1976.

White v. *Davis,* California Supreme Court, 13 Cal. 3rd 757, 1975.

Wilson, G.T. 1961. An analysis of effective practices employed to reduce vandalism in park, recreation and combined departments in American cities of over 50 thousand population. Doctoral dissertation, Indiana University, Bloomington.

Wilson, J.Q. 1976. Crime in society and schools. *Educational Researcher* 5:3-6.

_____. 1975. *Thinking about crime.* N.Y.: Basic Books.

Winston, P. 1974. Student involvement cuts vandalism: South San Francisco Unified School District. *School Management* 18:24.

Wint, J. 1975. Contrasting solutions for school violence: The crackdown. *Phi Delta Kappan* 57:175-176.

Wise, B. 1977. School security can be cost effective. *Educational Economics* 2:16-19.

Wolfgang, M.E. 1977. Freedom and violence. In *Violence in schools.* ed. J.M. McPartland and E.L. McDill, pp. 35-42. Lexington, Mass.: Lexington Books, D.C. Heath and Company.

Yankelovitch, D. 1975. How students control their drug crisis. *Psychology Today* 9:39-42.

Yerba Buena High School. 1975. *The Yerba Buena Plan: Solutions to conflict and violence in the schools: A school-based interagency team approach.* San Jose, Calif.

Young, G.P., and Soldatis, S. 1970. School vandalism can be stopped. *American School and University* 42:22-23.

Zeisel, J. 1974a. *Schoolhouse—designing schools to minimize damage from vandalism and normal rough play.* New York: Educational Facilities Laboratory.

_____. 1974b. Planning facilities to discourage vandalism. Paper presented at American Association of School Administrators Annual Convention, Atlantic City, NJ.

_____. 1975a. *Analysis to reduce property damage in schools.* Cambridge, Mass.: Architecture Research Office, School of Design, Harvard University.

_____. 1975b. *Annotated bibliography: school crime.* Cambridge, Mass., School of Design, Harvard University.

_____. 1976. *Stopping school property damage. Design and administrative guidelines to reduce school vandalism.* Arlington, Va.: American Association of School Administrators, and the Educational Facilities Laboratories.

Zimbardo, P. 1970. A social-psychological analysis of vandalism: Making sense of senseless violence. ONR Technical Report. Washington, D.C.: Office of Naval Research.

_____. 1969. The human choice. Individuation, reason and Order Versus Deindividuation, Impulse and Chaos. Nebraska Symposium on Motivation, 1969.

Zweig, A., & Ducey, M. 1976. A pre-paradigmatic field: A review of research in school vandalism. Chicago: Institute for Juvenile Research.

Index

Accountability programs. *See* Offender-accountability programs

Acquisitive vandalism, defined, 5

Ad Hoc Vandalism Committee (Madison, Wisconsin), 56, 57

"Adolescent identity crisis," 3

Aichorn, August, *Wayward Youth*, 3

Alarms: detection, 25–28, 91; local, 25, 91; personal, 26; silent, 24–25

Alexandria, Virginia: creation of, 61; impact of, 62–63; operation of, 61–62; prevention program in, 51, 61, 65

Alternative Schools Project, 77

American Association of School Administrators (AASA), Educational Facilities Laboratory for, 75–76

American Institutes for Research (AIR) Study, 12

Anderson, J., 17

Annual Register of Grant Support, The, 77

Architectural-design programs, 38–39, 90

Asbury, H., 1

Assessment, problem, for school-vandalism-prevention program, 67–76

Audio detectors, 26

Baltimore City Public Schools, 4

Bartlett, K., 16

Bates, W., 16

Baughman, P., 4

Baxter, J., 20

Beautification programs, school, 38–39

Behavioral-change programs, 41–43, 90

Berger, M., 46

Bischoff, William J., 52

Blauvelt, P., 5, 27, 30–31, 34–35, 70, 91

Borland, Glen, 56

Bradley, C.E., 14, 17

Brown College, 1

Business and Education Coordinating Council (Madison, Wisconsin), 56–57

Carpenter, J.B., 45

Cavan, R., 48

Center for Law and Education (Cambridge, Massachusetts), 48, 84

CETA, 34, 62, 64, 76, 77, 78

Chilton, R., 16

Clinard, M.B., 16

Closed-circuit television, 26

Cloward, R.A., 3

Cohen, S., 5, 19

Colver, A., 42–43

Community Development and Housing Program, 77

Community-relations programs, 45–46, 90

Community security, 32–33

Constitutional Rights Foundation (Los Angeles), 48

Contract personnel, use of, for security, 30–31

Controlling Crime in the School, 84–85

Costs: acquisition, 80–81; and financial gains, 82–83; operational, 81–82; of school vandalism, 5, 11–13; of school-vandalism-prevention program, 79–83

Council of the Great City Schools, survey conducted by, 6–7

Counseling, 43–44

Coursen, D., 28

Crisis counselors, 43

Curriculum-innovation programs, 47–48

Dallas, Texas, prevention program in, 51, 58, 65; creation of, 59; impact of, 60–61; operation of, 59–60

Daniels, H., 18–19

Debuzna, C., 18, 20

"Defensible space," concept of, 38

Detection alarms, 25–28, 91

Discipline, student accountability and, 41

Diversion programs, 39–40

Division of Children and Youth Services (Escambia County, Florida), 64

Domestic Assistance Catalogue, 77

Ducey, M., 4, 5, 16, 18

Dukiet, K., 11, 14

Education Policy Research Institute (ERPI), 29

Education/probation liaison (EPL, Fresno County, California), 52, 53

Education Research Service, 11

Elementary and Secondary Education Act (ESEA): 1974 Amentments to, 2; Safe Schools Amendment to, 77

Ellison, W., 18–19

Ellison, W.S., 16

Emergency School Aid, 77

Energy Conservation Act, 77

Erikson, Erik, 3

Escambia County, Florida, prevention program in, 51, 63, 65–66; creation of, 63; impact of, 65; operation of, 63–65

Evaluation, program, for school-vandalism-
    prevention programs, 85; assessing pro-
    gram transferability, 86–87; assessing
    rival explanations, 87; determining
    whether change occurred, 85–86; judging
    significance of change, 86

Factory Mutual Engineering and Factory
    Insurance Association, 27
Federal Bureau of Investigation (FBI), 36;
    Uniform Crime Reports (1975) of, 4
Ferdinand, T., 48
Fleetwood, Marvin, 58
Flint, Michigan, prevention program in, 51,
    54, 65; creation of, 54–55; impact of,
    55–56; operation of, 55
Fresno County, California, prevention pro-
    gram in, 51, 52, 65; creation of, 52–53;
    impact of, 53–54; operation of, 53
Furno, O.F., 11, 41

Gingery, S.L., 19
Glueck, Eleanor, 1
Glueck, Sheldon, 1, 2–3
Gold, M., 14
Goldman, N., 19–20
Goldmeier, H., 4, 16
Goss v. *Lopez*, 83
Graffiti, defined, 5
Grealy, J.I., 4, 11
Greenberg, B., 4, 13, 16, 19

Haggart, S., 80
Hamilton, J., 18
Harvard University, 1
Human-relations programs, 43–44, 90

Ideabook (NIE's Joint Dissemination Re-
    view Panel), 85
Identification, resource, for school-van-
    dalism, 76–78
Ideological vandalism, defined, 5
Individual approach to understanding
    vandalism, 2–3
Ingraham v. *Wright*, 83–84
Institute for Political and Legal Education
    (Pilman, New Jersey), 48
Institutional-change programs, 46–47
Interior, Department of, 77

Juillerat, E.E., 3
Juvenile Delinquency Prevention and Con-
    trol Act (1968), 2
Juvenile Delinquency and Youth Offenses
    Control Act (1961), 2
Juvenile Justice and Delinquency Prevention
    Act, 1974 Amendments to, 2

Kett, J.F., 1
Klaus, D., 12, 13, 44, 48

Law Enforcement Assistance Administra-
    tion (LEAA), 38, 57, 61, 62; Office
    of Juvenile Justice and Delinquency
    Prevention of, 12; and School Resource
    Network, 77
"Law-in-education" courses, 47
Leftwich, D., 17, 18, 19
LeMaster, T.J., 63
Leone, Dennis, 61
Local alarms, 25, 91

McDill, E.L., 3, 18, 47
McPartland, J.P., 3, 18, 47
Madison, Wisconsin, prevention program in,
    51, 56, 65; creation of, 56–57; impact
    of, 57–58; operation of, 57
Malicious vandalism, defined, 5
Market Data Retrieval, Inc., 11
Marvin, M., 4
Mechanical detectors, 26
Microwave detectors, 25–26
Miller, W.B., 3
Morgan, J.B., 1
Motivational factors, school vandalism and,
    92
Mott (Charles Stewart) Foundation, 54
Murillo, R., 16
Murray, C., 3

National Association of School Security
    Directors, 11, 18
National Center for Educational Statistics
    (NCES), 12–13, 15, 18. See also *Safe
    School Study* (1977)
National Education Association, 11, 14
National Endowment for the Arts, 77
National Endowment for the Humanities,
    77
National Fire Protection Association, 14, 17
National Institute of Education (NIE), 4,
    12–13, 15, 24, 93; on closed-circuit
    television, 26; Joint Dissemination
    Review Panel (JDRP) of, 85; on protec-
    tive devices, 35; on security personnel,
    28. See also *Safe School Study* (1977)
National Organization on Legal Problems in
    Education (NOLPE): Topeka, Kansas,
    48; Washington, D.C., 84
National School Public Relations Associa-
    tion (Arlington, Virginia), 48
Newman, Oscar, 38
Nowakowski, R., 16

Offender-accountability programs, 39–41, 90

Office of Education (OE), 11, 12
Ohlin, L.E., 3
Olson, C., 45
Omnibus Crime Control and Safe Streets
    Act (1968), 2

Pablant, P., 20
Palmer, J., 18–19
Parent-Teacher Association (PTA), 77
Passive infrared detectors, 26
Patrols, student, 33–35, 91
Personal alarms, 26
Phi Delta Kappa (Bloomington, Indiana), 48
Planning, program, for school-vandalism-
    prevention programs, 78; assessing costs,
    79–83; building political support, 83;
    considering kinds of programs, 79; con-
    sidering legal problems, 83–84; man-
    aging program, 84–85; selecting goals,
    78–79
Play vandalism, defined, 5
Police personnel, use of, for security, 29–30
Policy, formulating district vandalism, 70
Polk, K., 47
President's Commission on Law Enforce-
    ment and the Administration of Justice, 2
Prevention programs, school-vandalism-, 51,
    67; Alexandria, Virginia, 61–63; Dallas,
    Texas, 58–61; Escambia County, Florida,
    63–65; Flint, Michigan, 54–56; Fresno
    County, California, 52–54; Madison,
    Wisconsin, 56–58; problem assessment
    for, 67–76; program evaluation for,
    85–87; program planning for, 78–85;
    resource identification for, 76–78
Problem assessment, for school-vandalism-
    prevention program, 67–76
Protective devices, 35–36
Public Service Employment Program, 77
Public Works Program, 77

Reimer, D., 14
Resource identification, for school-vandal-
    ism-prevention programs, 76–78
Restitution programs, 39, 40–41
Richards, P., 16
Richter, J., 42–43
Rights and responsibilities, students', 48
Rubel, R., 11, 13, 14, 41, 42, 72

Safe School Study (1977), 16, 22, 47, 73,
    74, 89; authorization for, 2; on building-
    security programs, 24–35; on character-
    istics of vandalized schools, 19–20, 93;
    on correlation between crime and school
    vandalism, 21, 93; definition of vandal-
    ism in, 5; on extent of school vandalism,

12–13; on location of school vandalism,
    17–18, 91; and National Center for Edu-
    cational Statistics, 15; and National In-
    stitute of Education, 4, 12–13, 15; on na-
    ture of school vandalism, 15; on offender-
    accountability programs, 39, 41; on
    parent participation in school activities,
    54–55; quality of, 11; on rate of school
    vandalism, 17; on target-hardening pro-
    grams, 37; on targets of school vandal-
    ism, 15; on trends in school vandalism, 14
SARBs (school attendance review boards,
    Fresno County, California), 53
Schafer, W., 47
School(s): beautification programs, 38–39;
    characteristics of vandalized, 18–20.
    See also Vandalism, school
School-Community Advisory Councils
    (Flint, Michigan), 55
School Product News survey, 36
School Resource Network, 77
Security gaps, uncovering, 75–76
Security personnel, 28–31
Security programs: building-, 24, 90; com-
    munity, 32–33; detection alarms in,
    25–28; local alarms in, 25; protective
    devices in, 35–36; security personnel in,
    28–31; silent alarms in, 24–25; and
    student patrols, 33–35
Shaw, W., 5
Silent alarms, 24–25
Slaybaugh, D.J., 4, 13, 14, 15, 18, 19; and
    School Product News survey, 36
Social Agency Coordinating Committee
    (Madison, Wisconsin), 56–57
Societal approach to understanding vandal-
    ism, 2, 3–4
State Insurance Fire Rating Bureau, 27
Stretton, E., 14, 19
Student-account programs, 42
Student patrols, 33–35, 91
Suburban versus urban school vandalism,
    18, 91
Supreme Court, 83–84

Tactical vandalism, defined, 5
Target-hardening programs, 36–37, 90–91
Task force, establishing vandalism, 68–70
Television, closed-circuit, 26
Trailer-watch programs, 33

Ultrasonic detectors, 26
Underwriters Laboratories, 27
Urban versus suburban school vandalism,
    18, 91
U.S. News and World Report, 11
U.S. Senate Committee on the Judiciary,

Subcommittee to Investigate Juvenile
   Delinquency of, 2, 8, 11, 16
Vandalism, school: approaches to understanding, 2–4; assessing impact of, 74–
   75; causes of, 92–93; and characteristics
   of vandalized schools, 18–20; conclusions about, 90–93; defining, 4–7; extent
   of, 11–13; location of, 17–18; motivational factors and, 91; nature of, 15;
   need for further studies of, 20–21; rate
   of, 17; scope of, 71–72; seasons of, 21;
   summary of, 89–90; targets of, 14–15,
   21, 74; trends in, 13–14, 72–73; urban
   versus suburban, 18, 91. *See also* Prevention programs, school-vandalism-
Vandals, school, characteristics of, 15–17
Vestermark, S., 27, 30–31, 34–35, 70, 91
Vindictive vandalism, defined, 5

Wade, A.L., 16
Wallace, L., 11, 41
Watson, B., 14
White v. *Davis,* 84
Wisconsin, University of, 58

Yankelovich, D., 16
Youth Action Center (YAC, Dallas, Texas),
   59–61
Youth Employment and Training Program,
   77
Youth Problems Committee (Madison,
   Wisconsin), 57

Zeisel, J., 3, 5–6, 37, 41
Zimbardo, P., 3
Zweig, A., 16

The Council of the
Great City Schools

The Council of the Great City Schools is a nonprofit educational organization representing twenty-eight of the largest urban school systems in the country. Membership is limited to urban public-school systems that have enrollments of over 70,000 or are located in cities with populations of over 300,000. The Council's purpose is to promote the improvement of education in the Great City Schools through research, legislative advocacy, and other appropriate activities. For more than two decades, the Council has been in the vanguard of urban education, advocating the cause of urban school systems.

Board of Directors

City	Superintendent	Board Member
Atlanta	Alonzo A. Crim	Benjamin E. Mays
Baltimore	John L. Crew	Grover McCrea
Boston	Paul Kennedy	
Buffalo	Eugene T. Reville	Florence Baugh
Chicago	Angeline Caruso (Acting)	
Cleveland	Peter Carlin	Joseph M. Callagher
Dade County	Leonard Britton	Phyllis Miller
Dallas	Linus Wright	Jill Foster
Denver	Joseph E. Brzeinski	Omar D. Blair
Detroit	Arthur Jefferson	George Bell
Long Beach	Frances Laufenburg	Elizabeth Wallace
Los Angeles	William J. Johnston	Kathleen Brown
Memphis	Willie W. Herenton	Bert Prosterman
Milwaukee	Lee R. McMurrin	Lois Riley
Minneapolis	Richard Green	Marilyn Borea
Nashville	Charles O. Frazier	Isaiah T. Creswell
New Orleans	Charles Martin (Superintendent-Elect)	Mack J. Spears
New York City	Frank J. Macchiarola	James F. Regan
Norfolk	Albert Ayars	Joseph H. Strelitz
Oakland	Ruth Love	Barney Hilburn
Philadelphia	Michael P. Marcase	Arthur W. Thomas
Pittsburgh	Richard Wallace	Elinor Langer
Portland	James Fenwick (Acting)	Forrest Rieke

164

City	Superintendent	Board Member
St. Louis	Robert E. Wentz	Donald W. Williams
San Francisco	Robert F. Alioto	Myra Kopf
Seattle	David L. Moberly	Dorothy Hollingsworth
Toledo	Donald Steele	Samantha Adams
Washington, D.C.	Vincent E. Reed	Bettie Benjamin

Samuel B. Husk, executive vice-president; Milton Bins, executive assistant and senior associate.

About the Authors

Michael D. Casserly is currently a research and legislative specialist with the Council of the Great City Schools in Washington, D.C., and a doctoral candidate at the University of Maryland. He has written numerous articles, reports, and studies on various aspects of schooling in urban settings.

Scott A. Bass received the doctorate in the Combined Program in Education and Psychology at the University of Michigan in 1976. As a practicing community psychologist in the Boston area, Dr. Bass has directed and participated in numerous research, evaluation, and program efforts in a variety of organizational settings. He is currently director of Centre Research, Inc., an organization providing direct, long-range support to institutions and individuals in the process of responding to social problems, and associate professor at the College of Public and Community Service, University of Massachusetts, Boston.

John R. Garrett, currently a managing director at Vladeck, Hinds, Garrett, Inc., a Boston-based consulting firm, received the B.A. degree from Antioch College and the Ph.D. from Union Graduate School. Dr. Garrett's major professional interests include planning, research-program development, and working conditions in education and social service. He has published widely in academic and professional journals in a variety of fields. Previously, he served with the United States Information Agency in Vietnam and with the Peace Corps in Africa.